The Wild Calling

BELIEVE IN WHAT YOU CARRY

UNITED HOUSE

SAVANNAH PRICE

The Wild Calling —Copyright ©2021 by Savannah Price
Published by UNITED HOUSE Publishing

All rights reserved. No portion of this book may be reproduced or shared in any form–electronic, printed, photocopied, recording, or by any information storage and retrieval system, without prior written permission from the publisher. The use of short quotations is permitted.

NIV
Scripture taken from the Holy Bible, NEW INTERNATIONAL VERSION®, NIV® Copyright © 1973, 1978, 1984, 2011 by Biblica, Inc.® Used by permission. All rights reserved worldwide.

ESV
The Holy Bible, English Standard Version® (ESV®)
Copyright © 2001 by Crossway,
a publishing ministry of Good News Publishers.
All rights reserved.

All Scripture quotations are taken from THE MESSAGE, copyright © 1993, 2002, 2018 by Eugene H. Peterson. Used by permission of NavPress. All rights reserved. Represented by Tyndale House Publishers, Inc.

ISBN: 978-1-952840-09-8

UNITED HOUSE Publishing
Waterford, Michigan
info@unitedhousepublishing.com
www.unitedhousepublishing.com

Cover and interior design: Matt Russell, Marketing Image, mrussell@marketing-image.com

Cover and Chapter Title Illustrations by: Maria Sivils, maria@unitedhousepublishing.com

Author Photography by: Emily Maine, @arrowgracephotography

Printed in the United States of America
2021—First Edition

SPECIAL SALES
Most UNITED HOUSE books are available at special quantity discounts when purchased in bulk by corporations, organizations, and special-interest groups. For information, please e-mail orders@unitedhousepublishing.com.

Dedicated to all the wild people who have gone before me, stand beside me, and walk after me.

Table of Contents

INTRODUCTION 9

1. RAISE YOUR HAND 13

2. LOOKING FOR LOVE IN HEAVENLY PLACES 21
    The Unconditional Love of God 25
    The Steadfast Love of God 28
    You are Free 31

3. OUT OF MY MOUTH 35
    The Art of Remembrance 40

4. WHEN ANXIETY WRECKS THE PLAN 43
    Dancing Through the Flowers 47

5. OUR FREEDOM 53
    Dirt and Grace 56

6. TURNING POINTS – APATHY INTO ACTION 59
    Move your Feet 62

7. SURRENDER YOUR PLANNER 65
    What Happens When You Hit the Wall? 69

8. LET'S STOP THE FIRE TRUCK 73
    Finally, Let's Take A Nap 76

9. REST FOR THE WEARY 79
    Juice Cleanses and Jesus 82

10. WORK AS WORSHIP 89
    Holy Hustle 92
    Hustling Alone Isn't the Answer 93

11. THE BRICK WALL 97
    Abundance is Scary 99

12. BRAVERY IN HARD AND HOLY SPACES 103
    Holy Space 105
    When tragic circumstances arise, look for Jesus 109

13. SHAME ISSUE 111
    Healing happens when you believe fear has to go 113
    Healing Doesn't have to Make the News 115

14. STRENGTH 117
    I'm not everyone's cup of tea, but I might be their Vashti 121
    Let It Rain 124

15. THE THRILL OF HOPE 129
    He is with Us 132
    Though the Seasons Change 135
    God Doesn't Make Garbage 137

16. NEW YEAR, NEW ME 143
    The Banner of Truth 146
    Identity Crisis 150
    Lost in the Woods 154
    Less is More 157

17. BEAR WITNESS 159

18. WHERE ARE YOU STAYING? 163
    Come and see! 166

19. IT ALL MAKES SENSE 169
    Waiting on God 175

20. WHY WE NEED TO BLOOM 179
    Let's get ready 182

21. A NEW LEAF.. 191
22. FREE INDEED... 197
Final Thoughts 205
THANK YOU'S: 207
Notes 209
About the Author 213

INTRODUCTION

The gospel is not a tale of safety. Rather, it's a tale of fierce and wild love that God displayed to His people throughout time. Jesus was not sent here to make us safe. He came to make us holy. When we play the gospel safe, we strip our lives of the value that God has placed on it through His wild calling by shrinking ourselves down to the place where we are comfortable. Our callings are not supposed to be comfortable, but rather, they are wild. The reason is this: our calling looks dangerous and adventurous to a lot of people who don't believe in God's seemingly reckless salvation plan for us. The term reckless is difficult for some people to associate with an all-powerful God, but I don't mean it in a non-caring way. I think God's salvation plan was reckless because He took a group of people who deserved to die, sacrificed His own Son who is holy and blameless, and flipped the tables on sin forever. If that isn't wild, I don't know what it is. Now, you might find yourself wondering; who are these wild-calling people, and how do I become one? The good news is that wild-calling people are living for the Gospel, and by following the words of Jesus, we can learn how to do that as well. Wild-calling people have nothing to prove to the world or themselves. Wild-calling people are tired of playing it safe and living their lives shepherding their insecurities. Instead of living life in fear, wild-calling people are dancing recklessly through the fields of God's open grace and glory, shouting their praise (Romans 5:2). If your heart stirs when you read this description, then yes; the wild gospel calling is for you.

Welcome to the messy adventure I call the "wild-calling life" and the small portion of it I have been blessed to write about in this book. Maybe you picked up this book because you saw the pretty cover, maybe the title caught your eye, or perhaps you're looking for the joy and freedom others feel when pursuing what God has for them. For whatever reason you came to this page, welcome.

Please know your heart is welcome here. Let your hair down or keep it up. Read this book with your Bible and bullet journaling supplies, or pull it out of your bag during your kid's soccer practice. How and where does not matter at all. I would recommend at least a pen or pencil (or crayon, whatever you can find) because there are a couple of questions in each chapter to help you apply what I've said through the course of the pages. However you approach this book, know that you are cherished for your honest search for joy in whatever season you are discovering. We all walk through times of joy and periods of pain, but when we go through those things, we are called to be a lighthouse for someone else, guiding them into a safe harbor from their storm. This book is not my prideful shout but my small and steady beam of light onto some very rough waters.

I'd like for you to remember one thing: when people grow, they often compare their growth to others, but this isn't healthy or holy. Please breathe deeply. Let Jesus show you things for your life as you read and know everyone is at a different place, even if their interval of life looks similar from the outside. If anything I say in the following chapters helps you hear the voice of the Lord in a clear or new way, then all the glory is to Him. I am just a small piece in a very large body, thankful and grateful to help a fellow follower of Jesus.

I wish I could go back to being a freshman in high school, where all the world was shiny, and my fears were unclaimed. I wish I could go back to being a college student, feeling God's call on my life but being too scared to chase it with wild abandon. I realize that while the Lord didn't give me a time machine, He gave me this book to pass along to someone in a similar place in life. If you're doubting the call that God has on your life, this is for you. If you're sure of God's call on your life and want to encourage others along the way, this book is for you. The Christian life isn't a safety net, but rather a cannon, hurling us to the next beautiful thing to which God has called us.

You belong exactly where God has placed you, doing exactly the things you are passionate about, and helping exactly the people He has placed around you. If lies and fears are holding you back, allow God's Word to shine through and believe the plans He has for you are so good and beautiful. Enjoy this book, not for any wisdom I claim to hold but for the glorious unfolding the Lord will do in your heart while you prayerfully read the words this book contains. I am honored to even play a small part in your wild calling. Romans 5:1-5 (MSG) beautifully conveys the hope I want to pass along to you through this book. May you live your life in such wild abundance that the only thing you search for is more containers to hold His generous outpouring of blessings.

> *By entering through faith into what God has always wanted to do for us—set us right with him, make us fit for him—we have it all together with God because of our Master Jesus. And that's not all: We throw open our doors to God and discover at the same moment that he has already thrown open his door to us. We find ourselves standing where we always hoped we might stand—out in the wide open spaces of God's grace and glory, standing tall and shouting our praise. There's more to come: We continue to shout our praise even when we're hemmed in with troubles, because we know how troubles can develop passionate patience in us, and how that patience in turn forges the tempered steel of virtue, keeping us alert for whatever God will do next. In alert expectancy such as this, we're never left feeling short changed. Quite the contrary—we can't round up enough containers to hold everything God generously pours into our lives through the Holy Spirit!*
> Romans 5:1-5, MSG

CHAPTER **1**

RAISE YOUR HAND

Paying attention when God wants you to say, Yes!

Spiritual funks are no joke. I found myself in one recently, and no matter what I did, I couldn't figure out why. It wasn't like I was running from God; I was doing what I thought I was supposed to be doing. I was in a place in my life where I felt a lot of fulfillment. But something had settled in my bones, a funk, and I couldn't discover what it was or where it was coming from. I was surrounded by loving friends, a great support system, and lots of encouragement. For the life of me, I could not pull myself out of this funk.

Through a lot of prayers, counseling, and wonderful spiritual friends, I reached a conclusion: I had surrounded my thoughts with affirmations of over-sufficiency in areas where I thought I was the best, or thoughts of being unqualified in areas where I was fearful. These two thought circles had started to tear each other apart, leading to extreme spiritual exhaustion and a feeling of being off-track. I peeled back the layers and realized I had fallen into a pattern of self-dependence and comparison. I had told myself that others were doing more, and they were doing it better than I was. I got so caught up in what I felt I should be doing, I missed the fact that my pride was sustaining my calling. Bob Goff says it like this: "The way we deal with uncertainty says a lot about whether Jesus is ahead of us leading, or just behind us carrying our stuff."[1]

The Wild Calling

I sat in a lecture hall bouncing, full of energy and zeal for the upcoming semester. I was a recent high school graduate, and this was my first semester at college. My morning literature class had me bounding with joy. I started out college as an English major, and while God has shifted that goal, I've always come back to my love for writing. That first class was magical, the professor, informative, but not droll, and I walked away with confidence. I knew what I was doing. This class would be an easy *A*, and I felt about ten feet tall walking out of the lecture hall. My next class was Introductory Calculus. This, naturally, would be an extension of what I had learned in high school (or so I thought). I soon realized I was in a room packed with people who all appeared smarter than me. I know that's not a real thing, but they all just *looked* smarter; you know? It was the way they carried themselves that automatically made them worthy of academic prowess in my eyes. I sank low in my seat, forgetting that just moments ago, I was on cloud nine from the beautiful joy of my Literature class. My anxiety took over, and I allowed the enemy to pierce my heart with the lie that I was not good enough to be in the room. That Math class was brutal for me, and I actually failed it by three points. I think it would have been a lot easier to fail by thirty points, but I was determined to make every study group, teacher's hours, and beg my way to a passing grade. The one thing I failed to do was raise my hand in class.

I have always struggled with asking for help in front of a group of people, and that cost me the class and the grade I desired. If I had just raised my hand instead of comparing myself to my other classmates, I could have at least understood what the teacher wanted and passed the class. I've figured out my low opinion of myself in that subject versus my classmates' views of themselves was what sealed my fate. When I refused to raise my hand, I basically told myself I didn't need to know the direction the teacher was taking the class, and I was good enough to figure it out on my own. In order to soothe my wounded pride, I chalked it up to a bad teacher and moved on.

Over the years, I transitioned between three different majors, which meant I ended up with a completely different degree. I actually graduated with a Bachelor of Science degree that had required three years of Math. Looking back, I remember that first semester and the things God taught me, especially when it came to saying yes to what He was calling me to do.

RAISE YOUR HAND

I have come to firmly believe God used that first semester class to teach me more than any of the classes did the other three years. My mindset at the beginning of the Math class was that I was always going to be right, but when things didn't go my way, it caused serious heartache. I had tied my identity too tightly to how well I did in the class instead of to my Heavenly Father and His great love for me. When I rely on being right and succeeding as much as I rely on my love for Jesus, I step onto dangerous ground. This goes further than just the freshman year of college for me; it carries on into my everyday life. When I am eager to raise my hand to answer all the questions life has for me, instead of waiting on Him to direct my steps, I run the risk of committing myself to something out of pride, not out of calling. When I fail to raise my hand to say yes to His call, I can miss out or take the long route toward His great plans. While my Science degree wasn't something I anticipated, it was something God had called me to. God taught me that if I carry a high opinion of myself, my plans will most certainly crumble, but if I carry who He says I am, I'll walk in His confidence, not my own.

In my effort to "fix" this spiritual funk I had found myself in, I ran to Scripture like a kid searching for buried treasure. I desperately needed a reminder of my calling and that the One who called me holds all of the answers. I went looking for affirmation that I was doing what I "should" be doing and instead found the words of Jesus urging me to rest.

As Jesus and his disciples were on their way, he came to a village where a woman named Martha opened her home to him. She had a sister called Mary, who sat at the Lord's feet listening to what he said. But Martha was distracted by all the preparations that had to be made. She came to him and asked, "Lord, don't you care that my sister has left me to do the work by myself? Tell her to help me!"

"Martha, Martha," the Lord answered, "you are worried and upset about many things, but few things are needed—or indeed only one. Mary has chosen what is better, and it will not be taken away from her."
Luke 10:38-42, NIV

Jesus and I have a tricky relationship with rest. As a kid, I was praised for what I

"did," so I tied my worth to constantly being busy and active. I realized I should have been sitting at the feet of Jesus. I had allowed insecurity to carry me for so long that I was raising my hand to every opportunity that came my way, and my calling had been reduced to "doing good and sleeping when I can." This was neither holy nor healthy, and I believe my funk was less of a funk than burnout. In getting caught up with what I "should" be doing, I believed the lie that I needed to carry my calling, as well as every other miscellaneous thing that arose. Jesus does not tell us to be the best busy Christians we can but to come and sit at His feet and soak in His presence. Only then will we learn what we should do.

It's easy to get caught up in what you "should" be doing. Bills are always going to be due, people are always asking for your attention, and in the thick of it all, we're supposed to figure out what God has for us. It can be hard at times to realize what He wants you to say *yes* or *no* to, but listen closely: His heartbeat is the only tempo you're ever called to follow in this life. Instead of worrying about what the world wants you to do, are you actively paying attention to what God wants you to say *yes* to? If you are, that's amazing! If it's still something you struggle with on a daily basis, hang on. Jesus is not finished with you or me yet, friend. It is worth paying attention to His calling.

I recently met a friend for coffee and was telling her about a career possibility that was in front of me. I had the chance to lay down a more stable career to chase my dreams, but I was stuck with which choice I should make. I shared my fears, my joys, and really weighed what decisions I should make. Her response was, "Have you ever stopped what you're doing and realized you have a huge opportunity in front of you?"

I stopped in my tracks. See, it wasn't the first big opportunity that had presented itself to me that month. I had found myself with two giant opportunities, and I wasn't sure which one I was supposed to choose. I asked the Lord for strength to do both instead of a discernment to choose one. See, I was so used to managing it all, I hadn't even considered I wasn't supposed to carry both things full time. God gently reminded me my willingness to say *yes* to both things was amazing, but He didn't create our lives in such a fashion for the level of chaos that starting a new career full time and managing my own company would entail.

RAISE YOUR HAND

I had options and a choice to make.

That terrified me, if I'm honest. How was I to know what to choose? How was I to know which one God wanted me to pick? If I picked the wrong thing, would God still bless it?

Maybe you are in a stage of choosing between some big options; where to go to school, what career to pursue, or even what dream to follow. It's terrifying, but ultimately, God is calling us to only say *yes* to what He has for us. Sometimes, that looks like saying *no* to what others want for us. Sometimes, it looks like saying *yes* to multiple things. When we say *yes* to what God has for us, all other decisions are clear. When our lives are filtered through the lens of the Holy Spirit's discerning power, we find that the pressure is off of us. But how do we do this practically? Psalms is one of my favorite books to read, and during times of trials or decision making, I can find rest in the promises the book holds.

No one who hopes in you will ever be put to shame.
Psalm 25:2, NIV

Human nature has us make a lot of decisions out of fear, but as believers, we find strength in the decisions that come from the Lord. He will never lead us astray, put us to shame, or crush our hope. Just like the Psalm says, we have assurance God is working on our behalf. These truths are wonderful reminders, but in order to practice them in our everyday lives, we have to put them into action. When I was faced with a decision between two wonderful things, I dug deep into spiritual history and found something incredible: Jewish people read the Torah on a cyclical basis. Over and over again, they surround themselves with God's law, His nature, and truths about who He is to them. When reading God's Word, they start fresh every year so that they can surround themselves with His promises on a yearly basis.

Saying *yes* to God is like reading from the Torah. We can skip ahead to the part we're at now, but we get the most benefit from starting at the beginning each time. The confidence to say *yes* to what God is calling you to do can be found in the pages of your spiritual history. What has God done in your life that is worthy of remembering? Is there a miracle, a promise fulfilled, or a personal

The Wild Calling

testament of His goodness in a season of pain?

In order to say *yes* to what He has next for us, we must learn to count the fruit of previous stages. When we remember what God has done, our recollections become battle armor, strengthening us for the next day or stage of life.

Do you know what God has done in your life? This is one of the main reasons I'm such a huge advocate of journaling. Being able to flip through my middle school, high school, and college years to see how God has protected and provided for me gives me strength to say *yes* to what He's doing now. Count the fruit of what He's doing in your life currently, friend, and look back at old times in your life. You'll be amazed with what He's done.

I urge you to go through old journals and Bibles or sit down and reflect on moments in your life when God has provided, been faithful, and worked a miracle. Write these down, and put them somewhere you can see them as you get ready each day. Make it a practice to go over your spiritual history, and remember the goodness of God. When we pay attention to what Jesus is doing, everything changes. Romans 8:23-24 talks about how the Earth groans for us to realize what God is doing for us.

> *And it's not just creation. We who have already experienced the first fruits of the Spirit also inwardly groan as we passionately long to experience our full status as God's sons and daughters—including our physical bodies being transformed. For this is the hope of our salvation. But hope means that we must trust and wait for what is still unseen. For why would we need to hope for something we already have?*
> Romans 8:23-24, TPT

When we have hope in our salvation, we can't wait to see what God has next for us. It's like being a kid on Christmas morning, anxiously awaiting their presents under the tree. We have a creation-based longing to raise our hand for whatever God has next for us, but we often let the things of this world get in our way. For me, there was a crippling fear that I wasn't good enough, smart enough, or worthy enough. Therefore, I crammed myself into a box of things I knew I could do that were "safe" and didn't require me to ask the Lord what He had for me. When you shortchange your calling for the sake of comfort, you lose sight of the goodness of God.

I was raised in the church, comfortable with serving in the background, when God had clearly called me to lead. Through years of being wounded and letting the enemy's lies take over, I had convinced myself I was genuinely called to support and serve from the back of the room. Don't get me wrong; people who serve behind the scenes are incredible. There are so many things in the church and God's kingdom that go on behind the scenes. The Lord knows, sees, and loves each of those wonderful servants, and I am personally so thankful for them. However, my backstage serving came from a place of huge insecurity, and that does not honor the Lord. When I finally got the opportunity to serve in the spotlight, I wasn't confident enough to say *yes*! I eventually stopped serving in several areas because I felt if I wouldn't say *yes* to what God had for me, then I shouldn't serve at all. Sweet friend, I don't want that for you. I want you to raise your hand with a resounding *yes* and walk confidently into the calling God has planned for you all along. It's time to stop the negative self-talk and start letting the Lord supply your security. Walk out from behind the scenes and into the fullness of all He has for you!

The truth I learned in that moment, once again, came from Psalms, where it says: "Taste and see that the Lord is good; blessed is the one who takes refuge in him" (Psalm 34:8, NIV).

When we are ready to raise our hands, it first comes from recognizing the goodness of God. Seeing His goodness and realizing His security means we can live lives full of abundance instead of insecurity. There doesn't have to be some big declaration, but it can start with one small step. We can find our purpose by following Jesus, and all it starts with is recognizing His hand in our lives. Spend some time writing down what that looks like today, and allow the Lord to permeate every aspect of your fears. You are worthy of the calling He has placed on your life, dear one. You have to believe in the calling you carry.

Reflection Questions:

1. Describe a time in your life when you were in a spiritual funk.

2. What are some ways you deal with uncertainty?

3. Is there something God is calling you to do that you feel you are not prepared for?

4. How can you filter a big decision through the lens of the Holy Spirit?

CHAPTER **2**

LOOKING FOR LOVE IN HEAVENLY PLACES

I used to think the Holy Spirit lived in the rafters of my church. As a kid, I was fascinated with the theory that God looked down on us. Being able to see Him looking down at us the same way I saw my LEGO sets blew my mind and changed how I viewed Him. I saw God as an overlord, ready to pounce at the first sign of trouble but removed from His creation unless called upon.

With that said, God is tangibly in the rafters *and* on the ground with me. Heaven and Earth collide when we talk together. Creator joins creation, full of life, hope, and faith. This is *imago Dei*, (image of God), and my being made in the image of God doesn't isolate me from Him but instead, draws Him close.

I've always related more to the humanity of Jesus than to the seemingly isolated perch of His Father. God was cool and all, but He felt distant to me. Jesus got me; fully God and fully man. He more than likely stubbed His toes, experienced opportunities to get frustrated with His parents (even if in His righteousness He didn't), and probably had to make His bed every morning, which was basically like bearing my cross daily as an eight-year-old. With more years on me, Jesus became more of a friend, while God chilled in the distance. Over time, I started to realize God is writing my story in the kindest way possible, even if I don't see His hand on a daily basis. It took me until almost adulthood to realize that *imago Dei* does not mean the Creator makes His children only to

distance Himself to watch us walk through our lives alone. Instead, His heart is for us to learn to draw close to Him and hear His voice calling us to follow Him.

In order to do that in my own life, I had to stop looking at God as someone secluded and uncaring. I had to let go of the pride involved in figuring out my life on my own and be willing to spend time with Him to learn to hear His voice. My struggle was I had used pride as a barrier to create a "safe" distance between my life and my Heavenly Father. I thought if I kept ample space from God, He could never convince me to do anything I did not want to do. That worked for a little bit, but I found out I also pushed His love and provision away. Studying God's love gave me a grasp on what it meant to be made in the image of God and how to follow His wild calling on my life.

In order to discover the wild calling God had for my life, I had to first figure out who God is and what His characteristics are in relation to His people. The best place to find that is in the book of John, where there are a lot of discussions about love and the power God's love has in our lives. From commands to love one another, to examples of how to love, Jesus is clear to instruct the disciples with the different facets of the Father's love. Jesus' love for Mary and Martha was mentioned in John 11, and John 15 gives commandments for how we are to love. Today, we still struggle to see His heart, due to our limited concept of it. God's love is so much more than man's fleeting affection. Instead of God's love being compared to human affection, we are going to examine the multifaceted layers the Father's heart contains.

The first aspect for us to study is God's sustaining love. The definition of the word "sustain" in Greek means, "to support (mostly figurative) --comfort, establish, hold up, refresh self, strengthen, be upholden."[2]

When we look in the Bible, we see how God's love has sustained His children again and again. He provided manna from Heaven to nourish the Israelites. He provided refuge for David to protect him when he was running from his enemies, and He offers the same sustaining love to us today. This love is discussed by Jesus, in John 6, when He sees how the people are following Him so He will feed them. The crowd sought Jesus, but they sought Him for physical nourishment, not sustaining fulfillment. They were looking for His love in the form of being physically satisfied, but He was working towards so much more. Yes; He fed their bodies and met their physical needs, but He came into this world to save them (and us) from spiritual hunger. Instead of constantly chasing after the next meal, He wanted them to taste the Bread of Life. When we walk with Jesus, sometimes we chase after the small bits of food life offers us along the way rather than the ever-satisfying food He offers. The question we can ask ourselves today is, "Why am I seeking Jesus?"

Seeking God can come from a place of wanting to find Him, but it can also come from a place of benefitting from Him. We think we can trick the Lord, developing a "point system" in order to benefit from being close to Him. With this mindset, we equate the love of the Father to the provisions He gives us. When we work for the advancement of our own means, we never develop an understanding for the sustaining love of God.

Another thing I've learned when studying God's love is that the Bread of Life isn't about being wrapped up in perfect provision but being found in the presence of God. As Christians, our lives are wild adventures, but we can have confidence that even in the middle of storms, God holds us. As a kid, I hated storms. I would hide under my covers with my pillow over my ears, trying to block out the noise of the wind and rain. My dad noticed how much they terrified me and would try to teach me not to be afraid of them. He would bring folding chairs into our garage, raise the door, and sit with my brother and me so we could watch the storms from the safety of our father's lap. Eventually, I learned to love the storms and have been known to watch them from my garage from time to time. Whether the waves are crashing and the sky is pouring, or the sea is perfectly still, God is still holding us and will continue to hold us through every step of the way. We can find comfort and safety in our Heavenly Father's lap. The beautiful thing about the sustaining love of God is this: when we feel like we're set adrift on the seas of uncertainty or see storms of trial come rolling in, we can be sure we have an anchor who holds us to the very end.

The Wild Calling

Reflection Questions:

1. In what ways do you believe God's love has power in your life?

2. Share a time when you felt God disappointed you or let you down.

3. Can you list a couple instances in which you felt loved by God?

4. In what ways do you feel you love people well?

5. When it comes to loving others, do you feel you have more compassion for people you know or people you don't know?

6. Is there an area in your life where you wish you felt more loved by God?

7. Spend some time in God's presence in the next couple of days, asking Him to show you how His love is reflected in your life. If you struggle loving people well, read in the Bible about God's love for us, and put yourself in His shoes. Read 1 John 4, and take note of how many times love is emphasized or commanded. Write scriptures on notecards, or set reminders on your phone to love others as God has loved you, and see if you find yourself a bit more loving towards others after a couple of days.

The Unconditional Love of God

"As a prisoner for the Lord, then, I urge you to live a life worthy of the calling you have received. Be completely humble and gentle; be patient, bearing with one another in love. Make every effort to keep the unity of the Spirit through the bond of peace. There is one body and one Spirit, just as you were called to one hope when you were called; one Lord, one faith, one baptism; one God and Father of all, who is over all and through all and in all."
Ephesians 4:1-6, NIV

When Paul wrote this, he was appealing to the church of Ephesus to live as God had called them to live. Instead of acting like other people, especially non-believers, he encouraged them to honor God with all they were doing. Staying focused on our own calling instead of letting other people's opinions distract

The Wild Calling

us, could seem like it would cause hurt and frustration from others, but we can find true happiness when we follow our true calling. Have you ever battled the weight of trying to meet everyone's expectations of you? The people around you can have great intentions in their wishes for you, but somehow, you always let someone down.

This doesn't mean you're a failure, but you feel that way when the lights go down and you drift off to sleep at night. Instead of living for you, you spend your days trying to please the people in your life who you feel have some weight. The truth of the matter is this: those people love you, but they are human, and their love is conditional.

Our Heavenly Father's heart is full of purely unconditional love for His children. Examining the heart of the Father means we slowly begin to learn how to carry His heart in our own lives.

We are called to believe the calling we carry, as Paul mentions in Ephesians, but what does that mean?

As Christians, we believe God can use our lives for His glory. He does so by calling us in specific ways. Some people are called to be missionaries, pastors, stay-at-home parents, or business professionals. Each calling has value and is no lesser or greater than someone else's calling. We can be called and not have the tools or confidence to equip us in our calling, so that is where carrying our calling comes in. We can be called to do something and never respond to what God has asked us to do. However, when we carry it, it means we are actively pursuing the development and fulfilment of God's wild calling on our lives. This is when God's love is most evident and on display. God's unconditional love removes all the pressure the world puts on us.

It allows us to believe what we carry adds value and weight to our lives-not for pressure, but for meaning, belonging and purpose.

When we live our lives as unconditionally loved people, it starts to transform us. God's transforming love can remove hurts and disappointments, allowing us to live our wild calling unhindered. The transforming power of God begins to work in us when we not only see His love but incorporate its effects into our lives.

God's love can only enter your life as far as you allow your brokenness to be removed. When we hold on to past hurts, it is like holding broken glass in our hands. We can't understand why the wounds dig deeper. Why, when our Abba reaches out His hands to take our past shame and wounds, do we hang onto them for dear life?

I've been afraid that letting go of the wounds and the pain associated with them will somehow allow the hurts to happen again. I've been afraid to open up, to seek help, or to say *yes* to things because I used to be terrified I would not measure up or be qualified enough and would let God and others down. Instead of allowing God to hold me in my storm while I worked through my wounds, I hid from Him. The truth I learned is that storms will chase us, desperate to pull us under, but we are held fast by His steadfast anchoring. He does not call us to hurt us. The pain we experience is a result of a fallen world, not God's plan. He is holding my wounded heart, growing and healing it for His glorious calling. Something I've learned when discovering God's vast love for me is how He holds us when we feel we've been isolated or abandoned.

Our anchor holds us fast with love and draws us close with grace.

Reflection Questions:

1. Do you feel you've disappointed people?

2. Is there someone in particular you are especially afraid to let down?

3. How do you think that person would react if you let them down? Do you compare that to how you think God reacts when you let Him down?

4. How does your fear of failure translate into your relationship with God? Do you think you're less hesitant to move when you feel Him speak be cause you're afraid of letting Him down, or do you see God's unconditional love in your life?

The Steadfast Love of God

As much as the Cory Asbury song has made the theme of God's reckless love a popular topic, it is still an aspect of the character of God that needs to be discussed.

To understand the steadfast love of God, we also have to talk about the reckless component of it. When we compare the love of our Heavenly Father to the love of our earthly one, we get a skewed view of His love. Our earthly father could have done everything right, but ultimately, he is still human and makes mistakes. Our earthly father could have been distant, cruel, or even non-existent. The wounding we experience with our earthly father can quickly translate into how we see our heavenly one. Viewing God as an "untouchable" figure has led many of us to develop an idea He won't come after us; He'll just leave us where we are.

John 10: 9-10 tells quite an opposite story.

> *"I am the door. If anyone enters by me, he will be saved and will go in and out and find pasture. The thief comes only to steal and kill and destroy. I came to realize that they may have life and have it abundantly. I am the good shepherd. The good shepherd lays down his life for the sheep."*
> John 10:9-10, ESV

Jesus tells His followers He is the Good Shepherd, chasing after the stray sheep and leaving the flock to pursue the one that left.

If you've built an idea in your head that God is going to just let you wander away, you will find yourself wrapped up in His arms quicker than you can finish that thought. Though it won't be easy, He will never leave or forsake us. His promise to be with us means we will be protected, even in the storms of life; even in uncertain places. The Father won't abandon you, kick you out of the flock, or leave you out on your own in the wild.

Our Abba chases after us, whether we are in a time of wandering or a time of adoration, and He is quick to show us His immense love. He is furiously pursuing you, and whatever that looks like, He makes His presence in your life known. His reckless love doesn't mean He's careless, but He is intentional to create a divine encounter with His children. Immanuel, God with us, means Jesus came down from Heaven to redeem and restore us. We aren't going to be without trials, but we do have the promise God is going to work all trials for our good and His glory. He is chasing you, wooing you back to His heart, and at the end of the day, nothing else matters to Him but His children.

So, if you are feeling abandoned tonight, cast aside by the world, or even left out by the church, come back. Turn around, pick your head up, and hear your

Father calling out to you. In His pursuit of you, His love is steadfast and reckless.

Reflection Questions:

1. What does the word "reckless" make you think of?

2. Do any of those words relate to the nature of God? How?

3. How can God be both reckless and kind?

4. In what ways can you compare your Heavenly Father to your earthly one?

5. In what ways can you say your earthly father has taught you well about God's love?

6. Describe a time where you have seen God's love as reckless in your life?

7. Take a few moments and write down how you see God. Is He a stern father,

You are Free

"To the Jews who had believed him, Jesus said, "If you hold to my teaching, you are really my disciples. Then you will know the truth, and the truth will set you free." They answered him, "We are Abraham's descendants and have never been slaves of anyone. How can you say that we shall be set free?" Jesus replied, "Very truly I tell you, everyone who sins is a slave to sin. Now a slave has no permanent place in the family, but a son belongs to it forever. So if the Son sets you free, you will be free indeed."
John 8:31-36, NIV

The Jews were curious about the freeing love God offered through Jesus. It was hard for them to understand the context of spiritual freedom. Jesus taught them that being a slave to sin is just as bad as being physically enslaved by a master. At a point in my life, my biggest enslavement was to my schedule. I felt free time was a myth and I had to be the most productive Christian for Jesus to love

me enough. Instead, God asked me to give up my control and my enslavement to my schedule so I could learn more about His love for me. I learned so much about my calling in that season of life, and I encourage you to let Him free you as well. He invites us to no longer be slaves but to live out who we are as truly free people. The freeing love of God is what calls us to live full lives rather than crammed schedules.

There's a difference in a full life and a life full of striving. A full life is one overflowing with purpose, but a striving life is an overflowing schedule and an overwhelmed soul. Spotting the difference between thriving and surviving is discerning which way you are living, and if you are feeling overwhelmed, figuring out how to make the adjustments to a full life.

When it comes to our schedules, we believe a lie that God is pleased with us when we build our days full of doing things for Him, but in all reality, that's not what He's called us to do. Our Heavenly Father wants us to walk in His presence, fully known and loved, but without the anxious striving of a harried do-gooder, inspired by a list of accomplishments. This desire to please God with our actions and schedules might come from the right intentions, but the enemy can use it for shame in order to entrap us. The freeing love of God is the kind of love that liberates us from the shame we have carried for so long. We are so afraid of "messing up" in God's eyes, we stay in seasons we are supposed to move out of, stay around people we are called to walk away from, or choose things in life we think will satisfy us. Ultimately, the freeing love of God means we can mess up, and God loves us regardless. It's not a position of shame but a position of joy.

We can run into our Father's arms, get ahold of our Abba any time of the day, and then conquer anything we're facing in the world. As Christians, we get so caught up in the fact that God wants our very best, and He does, but by our standards, nothing will ever be good enough for Him. This is why God's grace and Jesus' sacrifice is so important. If there was not a way to be redeemed, we would be forever lost and alone. God's perfect standards are not achievable, but His grace is right in front of us. Though we have all sinned, we have all been redeemed. That's the wild story of the gospel. Our Creator sent His only Son to die for us so we can live abundant, grace-filled lives, pursuing the calling He created us for.

Instead of running towards the Good News, we allow fear to creep in and keep us frozen in place. It makes us sit in the corners of parties we don't feel invited to, even when the parties are thrown for us. We hide from the call of the gospel because we're afraid someone will realize we're just going through the motions. It seems safer in our eyes to be wrong with no effort, than to give it our all and maybe mess up.

Our Heavenly Father puts the scales away when His children approach Him. God isn't sitting in Heaven dwelling on all we do wrong; His heart swells at the thought of us. The freeing love of God allows us to walk in calling, knowing we're loved, and nothing else matters but God. Sit at the table knowing you are free today. Believe the wild gospel, and carry your calling, dear one.

If there is a pause in your spirit, or if you're exhausted, sit in the presence of Jesus for a little bit today with your schedule. Ask Him to pick out (or take off) things you should devote more or less time to. Ultimately, the Father is pleased when you are resting with Him, not running around anxiously.

Reflection Questions:

1. Did this week leave me feeling full or empty? Is that an indication of a root problem of sin?

2. What was your favorite part of the week?

3. In what ways can you ensure you feel rested and ready for next week?

Chapter 3

OUT OF MY MOUTH

I recently sat in a coffee shop working on some emails and just taking a break from the day, when I noticed something incredible and heartwarming. I saw a teenager and her dad come in for coffee, and as he bought their drinks, I noticed she looked at him with love, respect, and safety. They sat and talked about school, she even asked about his work, and they both laughed the entire time. For her, the kindness her father showed her by taking her out for coffee and asking about her life was way more effective than any lecture or demand from him.

I wasn't creeping on this precious father-daughter duo, I promise, but it did make me think of how we connect with our Heavenly Father. When it comes to Him, I think we often hear His commands but don't trace them back to His heart. We can come into our "coffee date" with God frustrated, impatient, or unwilling to communicate, and that can hurt our relationship with Him greatly. In my own life, I've been in places of doubting God's goodness, and it's made me more likely to cut our time together short or remove it from my life completely.

For years, I saw God as a commander rather than a Father, and it made me less likely to listen to what He was trying to call me to do. In all honesty, it had more to do with the position of my heart, and I wish I had figured out the reason for the commands sooner. I don't think God sits in Heaven and doles out unreasonable commands to harm us or hurt us, but I do think He asks us to leave things behind that are hurting us or could hold us back from our wild calling.

The Wild Calling

1 John 5:1-3 (NIV) illustrates this point, stating:

> *"Everyone who believes that Jesus is the Christ is born of God, and everyone who loves the father loves his child as well. This is how we know that we love the children of God: by loving God and carrying out his commands. In fact, this is love for God: to keep his commands. And his commands are not burdensome.*

God gives us commandments because He cares for us, and out of that kindness, we follow what He asks us to do. God didn't make robots; instead, He created children. This means He desires a connection with His creation and part of our calling is learning how to foster that connection for growth. One of the ways we do this is to look back and see how God taught His children, the Israelites, to have a relationship with Him.

From a young age, Hebrew children were taught to understand the Word of God and obey the voice of their parents. As God's children, we are called to obey our Heavenly Father, and obedience will bring us lives full of joy. As a child, I learned obeying my earthly parents came with benefits, but as a spiritual child, I learned it was so much more. Hebrew parents were extremely involved in their children's lives, and they were essential to the maturity of their children. The Hebrew language has eleven different words for children, with each of them describing different stages of a child's life. I love studying these different words and their meanings and think that by studying the stages of life Hebrew children go through, we can start to navigate the seasons of our relationship with God.

Words for children in Hebrew:

Zehrah: seed; practitioner of righteousness[3]
Bakar: first born[4]
Yanek: suckling[5]
Gamul: weaned child[6]
aph: child clinging to his mother[7]

OUT OF MY MOUTH

'owlel: child; boy[8]

lem: child becoming firm[9]

Naar: youth; servant[10]

Yathowm: fatherless child[11]

eled: son, young man[12]

Bachur: the ripened one; a young warrior[13]

> *Train up a child in the way he should go: and when he is old,*
> *he shall not depart from it.*
> Proverbs 22:6, NKJV

I first heard this Scripture preached at a child dedication, and it intrigued me. We train puppies to use the bathroom outside, we train cats to use the bathroom in a box, and we train children how to live their lives? I think I can master the first two, but the training children one is what gets me every time. I'm not a parent, and for years, I was terrified at the thought of my future children running around. Somehow, my lack of training them would mean their bad behavior would reflect poorly on me. While the internet is full of people who have no problem shaming others for their parenting shortcomings, having God as our parent means our failures do not reflect poorly on His nature. When I started reading the above definitions for how the Hebrews trained their children, I saw a similar pattern in how God had grown and trained me for different areas and callings.

Training children was something the Hebrews thought they had mastered, but throughout the Bible, earthly Hebrew parents failed their children because despite their best efforts, they were still sinful. How is this different from God training and growing us? God is perfect and fully divine, and He does not fail His children. When I started to dig, I found Hebrew "training" was so much more than teaching their children not to do something bad and to know the Torah. The word "train" in Hebrew, "hanakh," means "to initiate, discipline, dedicate, train up." The Hebrew synonym "hekh" means *palate* or the *organ vital for speech*. So when we are being trained, it's not just in the ways of right and wrong, but in the way we speak to others. The kindness God shows to us should directly translate to how we speak to others. Just as we are dedicated to the Word of God and learning His commands, we should also encourage others to pursue His kindness as well.

How do we encourage others to pursue His kindness? In a culture that seems bent on destroying kindness, while championing competitive spirits, we can make waves of change by following His commands. His Word says we are to lead by example, point to truth, and encourage remembrance.

Titus 1:7-9 says this to believers:

For an overseer, as God's steward, must be above reproach. He must not be arrogant or quick-tempered or a drunkard or violent or greedy for gain, but hospitable, a lover of good, self-controlled, upright, holy, and disciplined. He must hold firm to the trustworthy word as taught, so that he may be able to give instruction in sound doctrine and also to rebuke those who contradict it.
Titus 1:7-9, ESV

The art of growing as a child means remembering what the Father has taught us. One of the ways I realize the lessons the Lord has taught me is through daily communion. Daily communion is not the physical act of communion (Though, trust me, I'm always down for some bread!). It is the spiritual act of remembrance that physical communion provides. For me, daily communion looks like returning to the basics of a relationship with God and finding God there. It takes the pressure off of me to constantly create environments where I *have to* experience Jesus. Instead, it gives me space to experience Jesus. For me, it starts with something practical like making a cup of coffee while some worship music plays. Then, I take my dogs for a walk and return to read something from *The Book of Common Prayer* and a Psalm. Reading liturgy (a type of written prayer) allows me to center my mind and thoughts on who God is and on something rhythmic with which I have spiritual history. Psalms has always been a book that brought me closer to God, and reading it throughout the year gives me the opportunity to learn it better every day. If you've never practiced liturgy or repeatedly read a book of the Bible, I highly recommend it, simply for the consistency it gives your time with the Lord. It gives structure if you've never had a consistent quiet time with the Lord or if you find yourself distracted while

OUT OF MY MOUTH

trying to hear His voice.

Reflection Questions:

1. This week, try to plan a "coffee date" with God. Treat it just like you would an appointment with a friend, and use this time to talk with Him about anything on your heart.

2. In what ways do you feel pressured to create environments to experience Jesus?

3. If you have children, what are some ways you've watched them grow that could be compared to us growing in our relationship with the Lord? If you don't have children, use examples from siblings, cousins, or a friend's children.

4. What are some practical ways you can practice daily communion?

The Wild Calling

The Art of Remembrance

Once I'm centered on God's Word and His voice, I can better walk out my day. It's hard for me to imagine living my life unless it is filtered through Jesus, and while I'm not perfect, He most certainly is working to teach me better control of my words. The Father's calling on our lives isn't supposed to skip the social aspect of it. Our calling extends to our community. We can't engage in a healthy community unless we're willing to let the Lord work through us in our interactions with people. This is not always easy or fun, especially if there are difficult people in your life causing you significant stress.

As a child, I seemed to befriend difficult people. My mom would say to me: "God places difficult and unlovable people in our lives to grow something in us, and to someone else, we are just as difficult and unlovable." Ouch. I liked the first part of her words but struggled to hear I might be a difficult person to someone else. It made me cautiously consider my response before I was harsh towards others, and it made me pray harder for the Lord to show me the areas in my life where I was being difficult or unlovable to someone. However painful it may be to hear, we are not perfect, but we are made whole by spending time with Jesus and letting Him clean out the parts of our lives that make us hard to be around.

Some days, I struggle to allow Jesus to clean the difficult parts of my life. Whether it is pride or selfishness, I can have days when it's hard to surrender to the Holy Surgeon and His heart-cleaning process. On days when I struggle to love Jesus, I like to spend time meditating in His Word and remembering His promises. Like the act of communion reminds us of His sacrifice on the cross, my time in the Word with Him reminds me of His promises and love for me. On days when I struggle to love my neighbor, I take communion. On days where my loved ones or even I am a little less easy to love, I take communion.

This practice of remembrance is what makes my struggle holy. It brings me to a place where I have no choice but to fully rely on what God has done for me rather than what I can do for God. I can't be sanctified by my own body or blood; it's only Jesus who has that power. Finding God's kindness as we follow our calling is as simple as communion. The holy act of remembrance is what will push us to encourage others to pursue His kindness.

As children of God, speaking words of remembrance can remind us to whom we belong. Once we remember who God is and who we are, we must change the words we speak to match the calling we carry. Changing our language can determine whether or not we will live a life of joy or sorrow because the power of our words can change the lens through which we see God work.

Just as the tongue is vital for speech, the act of remembrance is vital to our walk with Christ. Learning to practice daily communion with the Lord is what will sustain us when we encounter the difficulties life throws at us. Once we've remembered how God has cared for us, it's essential we turn it around to others and teach the same to them. For many believers, it's impossible to actively practice remembrance when we are surrounding ourselves with self-doubt. By focusing inward, we only see what we have done and not what God has done in us. Believing what we carry means we shift our focus off of ourselves and onto the One who is worthy of all the attention. If our mouth controls our life, let's make sure God's Word is coming out of it. Surround yourself with God's truth, and make "a clean mouth" your prayer, just like the psalmist in Psalm 19:14 (NIV):

> *"May these words of my mouth and this meditation of my heart*
> *be pleasing in your sight,*
> *Lord, my Rock and my Redeemer."*

Reflection Questions:

1. What things in your heart do you struggle to let God clean out?

2. How do you see your words or others' words affecting you?

3. Do you have any negative, self-deprecating thoughts? If you've got a loop of discouraging words running around in your mind, write them below, and then pray God's truth over them. We can only fight the lies of the enemy with God's truth.

CHAPTER **4**

WHEN ANXIETY WRECKS THE PLAN

It started in first grade with standardized testing. I met my best friend because she was throwing up in the bathroom from test anxiety, and I was trying to splash cool water on my hives. We were instant friends, bonding in compassion for one another's anxiety. In middle school, my anxiety developed into nausea and constant fidgeting for me. When the popular girls looked my way, I twisted my hair into knots. As an adult, it looked like skipping breakfast, the constant need to be "doing" something, and my inability to fall asleep in anticipation of a big event the next day. I could write a whole book on what happens when anxiety takes over God's plan for my life. Sometimes, anxiety comes when my plan tries to trump God's perfect will for my days; other times, circumstances I don't foresee will end up taking over, causing me to spiral out of control.

"Do not regard your servant as a worthless woman, for all along I have been speaking out of my great anxiety and vexation." Then Eli answered, "Go in peace, and the God of Israel grant your petition that you have made to him."
1 Samuel 1:16-17, ESV

I'm not writing this book to say you just need to pray harder or love God more, and your anxiety will vanish; I'm saying I understand you. I've been with you on those anxious nights when you can't sleep. I think, as Christians, we sit with the idea that the dark parts of who we are actually mean there is something wrong with us. Instead of realizing God shows us things in every stage of life,

we allow our anxiety to scream from the darkness that we are never enough. Stopping that yell is the key to walking in our calling.

Normally, my anxiety comes as a result of two things. The first comes when I overwhelm my schedule, and the second when I isolate myself from community. When I isolate myself, all I do is bubble wrap myself in the enemy's lies. Then, I begin to believe I'm alone, and there's no one who will understand. Oftentimes, my anxiety creates my loneliness, and my loneliness feeds my anxious scrambling. I went through a season of life where I was a horrible friend. I was severely anxious, so I isolated myself to ensure no one saw me in that state. Many people were put off by that approach, but the few friends who stuck around, used their love as a battering ram to push through my walls. I had friends who let me stay at their houses and cry on the living room floor, friends who took me around town, driving with the windows rolled down, and friends who had the courage to pour beautiful truths into my broken soul.

The truths I have received for my anxious heart have become an anthem, and I'm going to pass them along to you.

You are not alone in your cave. However much this world is spinning, you wake up every morning, new and cared for by your Heavenly Father. Satan's lies have no authority when it comes to your identity, and your worth is not defined by how productive or loved you feel at the end of the day. God is good, and He is holding you.

Some mornings, I repeated those words as music, and some days, they were a battle chant. My anxiety had no privilege to wreck my soul, and as far as I'm concerned, it was an unwelcome guest.

When I was struggling with a huge amount of anxiety and depression and felt panicked, I started writing poetry. I wrote tons of poems in that time of life, but here is a favorite. When I get discouraged in my calling, I often lose track of what I'm called to do, but I've used this poem as a beacon of encouragement in times when I didn't see my calling. I pray that it helps you feel a bit lighter while you are walking your season.

WHEN ANXIETY WRECKS THE PLAN

You will not be lost here
In the blinking of the night
When the stars search for belonging
As you search for life

You will not be lost here
In the hustle when gas pedals carve your soul
And the hunger of the hustle eats like a mad dog
You search for hope

You will not be lost here
Just as babies cry for their mother
You watch waves cry out for one another
You will find home

You will not be lost here
There is healing and grace
Hope, peace, and joy
You have found yourself

You will not be lost here
As you set the keys on the hook
And the familiar smiles know your name
You are home, and hope lives here.

Your worth is not wrapped up in your anxious striving to do well. We will not, no matter how hard we try, be able to control things the Lord has willed to pass in our lives. Your anxiety is a state of belief, not a statue to run to at every turn of events. When you become anxious, process and release; don't build monuments to your fears. Anxiety is the weed that blooms when we desire to take control of our lives, instead of letting God have full rule. When we plant the idol of control too deep in our lives, it takes our nutrients, our energy, and our fuel, and it creates a monster, fueled by anxiety and fear. Instead of fighting the current, drowning under each wave, as it batters our hearts, allow Jesus to pull you above the wave to better things. You will not be lost here, dear friend. The Lord has His hold on you.

The Wild Calling

Reflection Questions:

1. What plans do you have for your life? Write down dreams, goals, and other accomplishments you want to achieve.

2. When you look at that list, does anxiety creep in? How does that affect your dreams?

3. When you feel anxious, what are your reactions? Do you isolate yourself or engage in community?

4. What is something you tell yourself when you are anxious? Could you possibly be repeating words of stress over your situation instead of words of truth?

5. What do you think God would label your current stage of life? Would He label it as full of understanding, as truth or as anxious striving? Take a minute each day when you feel anxious and sit in His presence. Journal some things you think He would tell you.

WHEN ANXIETY WRECKS THE PLAN

Read Hannah's story (1 Samuel 1), and try to put yourself in her shoes. Feel her loneliness, her pain, and her heartbreak, but watch how God shows up. How would you respond if you were in her shoes? Write down what your emotions, thoughts, and insights are when you read her story. God is a miracle working God!

Dancing Through the Flowers

One of the most significant (hidden) cries of my heart is to get back to dancing. I took ballet for a period, and while I'm not the most graceful person, I was one of the most committed. I would follow every step through, even the ones I knew I couldn't master, and when I fell, I would get up and keep trying.

One day though, I stopped trying. If we have been given the feet to dance, why do we stop? For me, it was because I believed I wasn't good enough, so fear kept me from doing the thing I loved most. Little did I know then, that was the precedent I was setting for my life and would follow to a bitter stopping point before the Lord cleaned out my heart. So many of us fight that declaration of inability, but on the days when the fight is too hard, and we give in, our feet stop dancing, and our hearts hear the lies of the enemy over the footsteps of our Dance Partner. I don't come to shame you for stopping your dance but to hopefully remind you that you still have feet, and they are made to move to the rhythm of our Creator's song.

The Wild Calling

You can be resisting your dance for a variety of reasons, such as fear, defeat, and anxiousness. For years, I fought so hard not to be like people in my life who had given up on their dreams. I watched them take the safe route out of fear. I was afraid I had settled along the way for things that were not God's best. Instead of claiming the victory Jesus had already won for me, I fought my family legacy of shame and defeat because I believed I was defined by it,

I have stories of drug addiction, alcoholism, abuse, and other horrible generational sins that have followed me on both sides of my family. When I was little, these things were hidden from me, a vault of old stories hiding a sinister truth. The enemy thought he had power over my future, and for a while, I believed him. I started saying things like, "Well, my grandad did this, so I'll probably have to deal with it later," and other similar things. My doctor visits were at least fifteen minutes of who had what cancer and which family member had heart disease.

I didn't realize until later I'd done the same thing with my legacy. I'd say things that would remind me of a family member, and I'd start to claim I was just like them. Instead of claiming victory, I saw the family tree turn into a web of crippling anxiety before my eyes. Instead of looking at the beautiful parts of my family and actively praying against the rest, I doomed myself right out of the gate. A dear spiritual mentor of mine shook me awake with the fact I was not the sum of my family history but rather the next chapter of it. I could write the chapter the same as the others, with doom and gloom, or I could allow the Lord to clean out the generational pre-dispositions and sin and write a story of redemption for the ages.

Your legacy can either cripple or propel you to greater things. So many of us fight our legacy because we believe prophecies over our destiny. It shows us where we are to carry the Father's heart. Because of my family members' struggles with addiction or substance abuse, I can watch more carefully the position of my heart when I drink or choose not to altogether. Out of their struggles with mental illness, I can actively take every thought captive and pray the Lord stands guard over my mind at all times. I have a huge respect for people with different stories than mine, but I have a special place in my heart for others who carry similar burdens.

WHEN ANXIETY WRECKS THE PLAN

I think, sometimes, the Lord allows us to see other people's choices up close, by making them our family, and their flaws scare us into running away from them completely because we fear we'll end up like them. I made up my mind I wasn't going to have a destiny of settling. This would only happen if I allowed fear to seep in and take over. I had been allowing fear to take over to become an anthem in my heart through my teen years until one day in college. It finally hit me when I heard a friend of mine talk about how she had overcome her family's cycle of addiction by releasing it back to God and trusting Him to control her fears, instead of trying to manage them on her own.

> *I could either live a life filled with balancing fear and safety,*
> *or I could recklessly dance, full of wonder, purpose, and joy.*

I learned in that time of life my idea of safety was not the same thing as God's plan for my destiny, and fear crept in when I confused the two. Instead of throwing me to my own devices, God, being so merciful and gracious, led me to some of the most beautiful women in the Bible who had overcome hard circumstances and learned to bloom and grow into who He had made them to be. The thing is, I made my life a lot harder because I hid my struggles and my questions. I was like a music box ballerina, twisting and turning but never really going anywhere. I hid my anxiety, my distorted self-image, and, ultimately, the fact I had settled for less than who God had created me to be.

One of the reasons I fell in love with Jesus all over again on this journey was reading about Ruth and Hannah and the beautiful fact they didn't hide their adversity. From Hannah's never-ceasing prayers, to Ruth's patience in God's timing, they were no strangers to waiting on God to work. We all struggle, but these women asked their questions and trusted God until they saw Him bring His promises to completion. Their trials and hopes were clearly represented in their lives, and it reassures us we all face difficulties in our own ways- from waiting on a promise to be fulfilled, to hearing God's voice in the middle of uncertainty.

Cleaning myself up before church, serving, or being a part of a small group was huge. No one could ever sense I had settled because, "I was just so happy to be there helping." The words, "What can I do for you?" became my mantra and

where I hung my self-worth at the end of every day. If I helped enough people, loved enough people who were visibly hurting, or did enough for the church, I was doing well. But instead of doing well, the small dancer in me kept shrinking and was never allowed to come out and show the world who I really was. Maybe, if I served enough, no one would ever catch on to the fact I didn't allow myself to be fully loved and known by anyone else, much less God.

The thing about hiding brokenness is, it's like sticking your finger in a hole in a dam; you're stuck there until one of two things happens: the dam could break, exposing all of the brokenness you've been hiding behind the walls, or it holds, and you continue smiling as people walk by. You wave at friends, and even encourage some in the midst of your "patch job." But that façade can only last until the water builds up too high, and all of your hurt comes flooding in, covering the people around you in your brokenness. When this happens, you can either retreat or emerge soaking wet, ready to get dried off and actually start again. Jesus made a way to drain the water, and it was not by having us dump enough buckets. It was by pulling our fingers out of the dams, trusting what He was calling us to do, and realizing we weren't created to stay stuck in our brokenness.

Reflection Questions:

1. What is something you gave up years ago that you'd love to get back to?

2. How can you determine to live a full life? Why? As Christians, we are called to experience fullness that comes from Jesus, but we often settle for the sidelines out of fear.

WHEN ANXIETY WRECKS THE PLAN

3. As Christians, do you believe we are called to walk in vulnerability? What does this mean to you?

4. Are there people in your life who know you through and through? They could be mentors, your spouse, your best friend, or even your mom. List those people here!

5. If you aren't being vulnerable with anyone, is there someone in your life you could open up to?

6. What is something you're afraid of, when it comes to being vulnerable? (Rejection, shame, jealousy, etc.?) Explain.

7. This week, find a person with whom you can be fully vulnerable. If you already have one, call them and meet, and open up to what the Lord is doing in your stage of life. If not, pray the Lord would highlight someone!

CHAPTER 5

OUR FREEDOM

There is freedom to be found in this season.

I wrote that in a journal several years ago, not knowing by declaring those words, I'd set myself up for a wild journey with my Savior- a time of growth. It also set me up for a ton of lies from the enemy. When I pictured freedom, I pictured a girl dancing through a field, nonchalantly, believing in her steps and who she was.

*What I didn't realize was in order to get through to my freedom,
I had to go through my fear.*

My top fears were based on other people's ideas of me. I had believed I was never going to be good enough, smart enough, funny enough, or kind enough to be fully known and fully loved. At the root of that fear was one even more toxic: I feared I was not worthy of love from God. He created me, He made me, but He messed up. I believed the lie that because I wasn't the size I wanted to be, as wealthy I felt I needed to be, or as well-liked as everyone else was, God saw me as a failure. Surely, He, like everyone else, equated my worth to the amount of love He'd give. I placed myself on an incredibly impossible scale that set me into a tailspin of fear, anxiety, and failure.

When I finally cried out to God; instead of taking me out of my situation, my anxiety, and my stress, He hid me in the middle of them. It was like when David ran from Saul and ended up in the cave of Adullam in 1st Samuel 22; I found myself in a very isolated refuge with God and God alone. Instead of appreciating the beautiful gift the refuge was, I banged against the walls in my spiritual hiding place, much like a child complaining about being sent to their room for time out. I became the ultimate child, convinced my Heavenly Father was punishing me, and I was angry at Him for every minute of it. As it is with every tantrum-throwing toddler, I eventually became worn out and crawled into my Abba's lap.

In those moments of complete silence, I found the Lord in a way I had never found Him before. I had always looked at God like a strict parent. An A+ was never good enough for Him, and I wasn't trying hard enough. But when I surrendered in my place of refuge, He pulled me close, and I heard His heartbeat. His heartbeat wasn't found in the worthless striving I had pursued before; it was found in the silent moments in the cave, the refuge with just Abba and me. When we are hidden with God, it might be painful, but it will bring so much joy and freedom, if we surrender. I learned that in order to be hidden, we have to be rescued from our current situations.

Friends, *rescued* doesn't mean the same as *removed*. You can be hidden with God in the tornado of your everyday life and feel disconnected from the situations around you. This can be an indication you're nestled safe in your Father's arms.

Psalm 18:19b (NIV) was a verse I would cling to during this time: "He rescued me because He delighted in me." He delights in me, not "tolerates me," "puts up with me," or "acts like He loves me." It's sheer delight. The definition of delight is to "please someone greatly."[15] I don't see a lot of disappointment wrapped up in that verse, do you? Sweet friends, we please our Father when we are hidden with Him. We are not a burden He takes out of obligation, but a joy He welcomes into His family. We belong in His family.

In that place of hiding, in that spiritual cave, I learned the truth that changed everything. My freedom didn't come from doing enough for God so He would love me, but from the security He delights in me as His child. There's freedom

OUR FREEDOM

to be found in knowing we can run into Abba's arms at any time, and He delights in our presence.

I've always wondered what it means when God delights in us; for instance, how does He show us His delight?

He gives us His perfect peace. When we experience a peace only God can give, one that surpasses all understanding, freedom follows. Through this freedom and the joy that comes with it, we are able to turn around and proclaim His goodness in our hidden space. When we are in this hidden place, we find freedom in knowing our Abba's heart.

This God--His way is perfect; the word of the Lord
proves true; He is a shield for all those who take refuge in Him.
Psalm 18:30, ESV

Reflection Questions:

1. Write Psalm 18:3, on notecards, and place them throughout your house. With God as your refuge, how can you begin to look at your situation differently?

2. Is there someone you know who has been in a similar stage to yours? Call them; ask them for coffee or lunch, and listen carefully. The Lord has etched something on their heart in that time of life that you need to hear.

3. I encourage you to read the story of Hannah, as we talk about freedom, and specifically note how she released her situation to the Lord and claimed His promises. As you read her story in 1 Samuel 1-2, look at the past couple question sections. How are you seeing God move in your life in the same way?

Dirt and Grace

Looking back on the story of Hannah, I'm reminded of something incredible. She could have accepted her "dirt" (her inability to bear a child), but instead, she begged God, never settling, and He rewarded her heart. She could have allowed her emotions to speak fear into her heart saying God was never going to provide, but instead, she believed He was always working. The things we allow our emotions to declare in our lives (thoughts like we aren't good enough or God isn't working in us) are nothing compared to the truths God speaks over us.

He calls us by name to a wild adventure. All we must do is say *yes* to this gospel calling.

So, here's the thing: a lot of you have been getting freed up from something through the pages of this book. If that's you, praise the Lord. He is so good. God frees us from something, but He also frees us for living our wild calling.

This book is a potential gateway for us to take home the freedom we've found discussed in these pages. If the Lord has given you freedom from something as you've read throughout the pages, hang on to the memory of that moment. Go back onto the dance floor with confidence. Have confidence not only in who you are but also in whose you are.

In Jess Connolly's book *Wild and Free*, she claims red lipstick gives her confidence. On her journey to being free, she stepped out and wore new clothes, jewelry, and most importantly, red lipstick. She had always believed she couldn't pull it off, but she realized she was believing a lie about who she was. I struggled for years to love who God created me to be, and I lived a lot of my life in fear. When God shook me and delivered me out of that fear, I started to realize I could go confidently in who he had created me to be. I realized if I wanted red lipstick, I was going to walk in freedom and confidence and wear some!

Here is your challenge. Stop at the store and buy some red lipstick. Or a new shirt. Or a new pair of shoes. When you get that item, put it on. Then, go back to your time of life, whether it's one of waiting or faithfulness, with it evidently displayed--remembering all your experiences and the freedom the Lord has worked in your life. Walk into your house and into your newfound freedom with purpose, confidence, and maybe some red lipstick. Know who you are, and that you're so loved.

Reflection Questions:

1. What tangible things in life give you an extra boost of confidence (like red lipstick or the perfect business suit)?

2. What has been your most significant takeaway from the past chapter?

3. What's been the hardest thing for you to hear/work on in this chapter?

4. Did you ever meet with someone and have a "vulnerability moment" with them? If so, what was your takeaway? If not, do you have plans to schedule one?

5. Write down any changes the Lord has led you to make in your life in the past couple of weeks.

CHAPTER **6**

TURNING POINTS – APATHY INTO ACTION

Do you ever just casually flip through your Bible, hoping for God to reach out and give you some miraculous word on what to do next? I used to be extremely interested in journaling and putting artwork in my Bible, but as I became focused on whether a page was "social media worthy" or not, I missed out on the blessings it contained. We can get so caught up in the aspects of the Bible that comfort or nurture us, we forget how to develop the part of our hearts that constantly searches for God's voice. If you're like me, know you're not alone in your searching.

That's where I found myself recently, and it is hard for me to come out of it. I had been in a funk with my quiet time. I was either reading a devotional or just re-reading something I've read a million times but not paying attention. I was stagnant but still seeking, and honestly, it was a frustrating place to be. I realized I had come to a turning point in my walk with Jesus while turning pages in my Bible. This season was not one of desperate seeking but one of learning and growing, which made me feel stuck. God was doing a whole lot of new things in my life, and while they were all growing at once, I felt lost. I found comfort by Zechariah 4:10a (NLT): "Do not despise these small beginnings, for the Lord rejoices to see the work begin…"

Just as God had a beginning for the world, He has a start for us. While we feel like His starts are small and slow, small starts have room for growth. When we

find ourselves in the in-between periods, it's easy to miss the growth because it's not extremely visible. Once you reach an in-between time with the Lord, it's easy to get frustrated and just stop. God tells us in His Word to seek Him, but what if we don't find Him on our timeline? Where do we go from there? I found myself searching for His voice, and by way of His voice, I can know my growth is happening, even if it is small at times.

There's a term in English literature called anagnorisis, meaning when a critical discovery is made. Oftentimes, it's when a character has been driving himself crazy to figure out what he needs to do next, and then suddenly, guidance appears, leading to a turning point in the story. That turning point is defined by the Greek word peripeteia, which means, a complete reversal in the story. Now, I don't want to get super technical, but I am an English nerd, so I love finding all these little things and applying them to my walk with Christ. Mike Rowe, the host of "Dirty Jobs" once gave a speech on anagnorisis and peripeteia, and in the speech, he claimed these terms are for "discoveries that lead to sudden realizations."[16] For me, the term peripeteia has been a declaration, a comfort, something to cling to when I get stuck in a place of aimless time with the Lord.

In the Bible, peripeteia is illustrated through Paul's conversion. Saul is someone who is so focused on his dreams, goals, and career aspirations, he misses God's call on his life. Nonetheless, when God declares Saul to be a "chosen instrument of mine to carry My name" (Acts 9:15, ESV), Saul receives a peripeteia moment and is forever changed. God not only gives him a new call, but a new name, and Paul goes on to write a good portion of the New Testament. If someone like Paul can experience a turning point in his story, be encouraged that God can take your story and turn it around.

My encouragement to you is in times that feel stagnant, keep seeking. What we believe will come to pass says a lot about who we believe God to be. How we walk this in-between season says a lot about who we believe God is to us, regardless of what we tell others.

In good days or bad days, it's not about us: it's for His glory. Our in-betweens are not lost on the God of the universe. While head knowledge does not mean heart action, it can be a catalyst to get our feet moving. When we tell God who

TURNING POINTS — APATHY INTO ACTION

He is, we start to discover who we are called to be in the in-between.

Reflection Questions:

1. How would you describe your quiet time with the Lord? Is it inquisitive or full of apathy?

2. Have you ever had a turning point in your life before? What did that look like?

3. What are you asking God for in this stage of life?

4. What do you think God is trying to teach you in this in-between place?

5. Do you feel like there's anything holding you back from moving into the next period of life, and, if so, is this why you feel stuck?

6. What are some moments of peripeteia in your life? Look back onto your spiritual history with the Lord and recount all the beautiful things He has done for you. What I mean by this is, where have you seen the Lord work on your behalf in your past? When you look back and see His working, can you see similar patterns in your season now?

Move your Feet

I felt like the wind had been knocked out of me. I had gotten hired for an impressive job in my degree field, was making good money, and working with a great team. My boss had given me a new project to run, and so I took the initiative to use what I had learned in school to make the most of the company's time and resources with the new project. My boss, however, decided the project was no longer worth pursuing and decided to shut the idea down. The perfectionist in me does not handle rejection well, so when I asked him about it, he very curtly replied he did not see any value in what I had done. As wounded as I was over the idea being rejected, I was unprepared to experience the wave of emotions that came next.

I found myself exhausted and ready to turn in my two-week notice. I eventually realized a few additional things about the job. The Lord was using it all to show me my time there was done. I had initially taken the job because my full-time passion wasn't as profitable as I needed it to be, and I accepted the position because I believed it was God's best for me. That led to a stage of being stuck because though my heart knew I was supposed to step out in faith and pursue my passion full time, my head kept telling me I would never make it. This made my soul feel like it was being torn between two mountains, leaving me stuck in a very lonely valley.

In the in-between, it's easy to feel empty and emotionally barren. Isaiah 13:2a (ESV) says, "On a bare hill, raise a signal." Even in the middle of bare land or an empty-feeling time, ask for help. There is no shame in coming to community in a season of weakness.

One of the things I realized was I had removed myself from people who knew my heart's desires. These people encouraged me to speak truth and follow God's calling for my life, and when I finally came around, they were waiting with open arms. I found myself speaking truth back into my life, and in turn, I was able to preach truth to others as well. I didn't have to pretend, but I began to speak truth even when I didn't feel its power. When Saul was converted and Jesus appeared to him, Jesus didn't tell him the plan for his life. He simply instructed him to "rise and enter the city, and you will be told what you are to do" (Acts 9:6, ESV). In turning point seasons, where you feel stuck, just get up and move. The Holy Spirit in you will guide you where to go, if you're willing to move your feet.

Psalm 139:8-10, says wherever we go, God is there. God's presence in our lives as believers is similar to the fire by night and cloud by day that led the Israelites through the wilderness. Instead of flames, God's Spirit burns in our hearts, leading and guiding us to follow His commands. We are called to "go," and after that, the rest is up to the Lord. I think one of the things that plagues us as modern-day Christians is we really don't have a ton of external motivation to follow the leading of Christ. When we rely on external factors to motivate us to move, or we come to a turning point in our lives, we can run into the distractions of this world. When you're looking for a command or a direction, *look up*, not out. The waves and storms of this world can pull us under, but looking for Jesus above it all, will keep us in forward motion.

When our eyes are fixed on the light of God's goodness, the truth of our purpose will gleam through any shadows. This revelation will lead to a turning point on our bare hill, and we can see clearly how good God's plan for us is. My encouragement to you today is that you start seeking His goodness, even from your bare hill. The steadfast love of the Father will lead you to your purpose. Just start moving!

Reflection Questions:

1. When you feel empty in your life, what do you turn to? Do you turn to a friend, an addiction, or a struggle?

2. What are some distractions you struggle with? Are there things taking you away from focusing on Jesus?

3. When you identify what is distracting you from Jesus, you can shift your focus back onto Him. Write down what you can do to focus on that in the next week. Whether it's a sticky note reminder, an accountability friend, or developing a new spiritual discipline, make a goal, and make it happen this week!

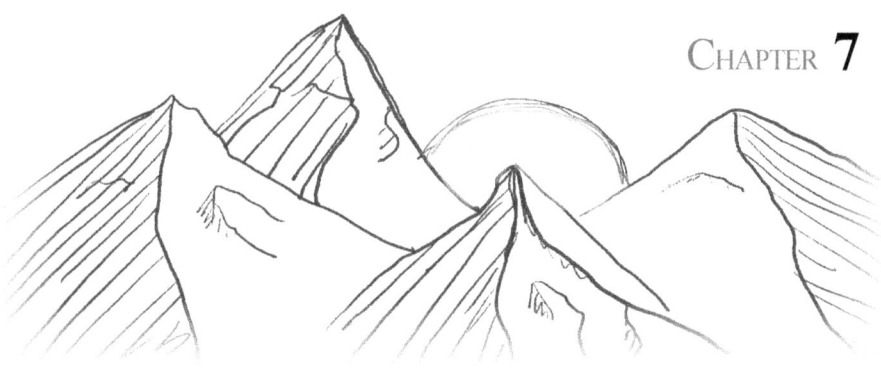

Chapter 7

Surrender Your Planner

As a kid, I loved back-to-school shopping. My favorite thing was to walk down the aisles of notebooks, pens, and planners and imagine how many of them I could use that year. I obsessed over the syllabi my teachers handed out, actively jotting down notes with multi-colored pens and aggressively bullet journaling before that was even "a thing." My insecurity screamed from this avenue, cheering for me to go onward because if I couldn't be the smartest, I could at least be the most well-planned. Eventually, I began to take on water in the sinking ship of planned perfection, and as I crumbled under this weight, I finally began to understand the importance of rest.

Actively pursuing rest is like remembering to take your medicine in the morning; it's hard to start but can be a lifesaver, with consistency. If you're crying out under the weight of over-planning, I ask you this question: What does this lifestyle of healthy rest look like for you? My encouragement to actively pursue the rest God has called you to is this: treat your schedule like an extension of your body.

If you don't have a planner, I highly suggest you get one. Some people use their phones; others prefer physical supplies. I honestly have loved and used both, but it's whatever works best for your life. When "planner season" comes around, I rejoice. I run to my nearest Target, grab some office supplies and a new planner, and go sit somewhere quiet, while I plan what God wants the year

The Wild Calling

to look like. I'm a bit passionate about setting good scheduling boundaries, but that only comes from having times when I wasn't organized, and I felt crushed under the weight of my own scheduled commitments and obligations.

Once in my life, I hit a period so hard I couldn't imagine God was in it. I was trying to achieve so many things in my own strength and power, I simultaneously ran myself ragged. I was a full-time college student, commuting to school every day, working two jobs, and going to night classes to get my real estate license. Needless to say, I was exhausted and utterly overwhelmed with everything I was trying to cram into my days to make myself the perfect girl. In a period of frustration, I broke down the persona that I'd created and let the Lord sweep in. It is only by His mercy I am here today.

Does this girl sound like you at all? I jotted this girl's description down one day between ill-planned overlapping activities.

Here's to the girl who has it all together.

She's got the work-life balance, the social life, the man of her dreams, and a perfectly curated Instagram feed.

But she's exhausted. Eyeliner is gone halfway through the day from either stress, tears, or chronic allergies she won't take care of; she has more coffee than blood in her body, and she may fall asleep as soon as she sits down, often while scrolling on her phone.

Girl, I see you.

That girl is me. For years, I've played my cards right to get everything I want, so it looks like I have the perfect life. In my mind, I'm so perfect, I've even been investing in the stock market recently. Fiscal responsibility equals perfection, right?

But I'm worn out. I'm ready for the invitation Martha rejected. I'm ready to sit at Jesus' feet. Martha neglected time with the Lord to get things done, and her desire to be the best made her extremely lonely. The struggle for perfection is

SURRENDER YOUR PLANNER

isolating, and this is the day we start breaking walls down.

First, let's start with some hard truths. My curated feed has made my soul empty, and a full schedule has trashed my ability to rest.

Someone asked me where my margin in my schedule was to take a break; and honestly, I could not answer. They went on to say they scheduled everything with twenty-to-thirty minutes in between appointments or activities so they'd have plenty of margin, and if I'm honest, I was a bit jealous. Truth be told, my margin for a break in my schedule had run off in the distance when I took on the mantle of pulling my life together on my own. I had days of rest, but they were filled with scrolling through Instagram or cranking out a blog post. They were filled with car washes, vacuuming, or a never ending pile of laundry. I've come to this realization from a season of being margin-less: *Just because you've slowed down from one-hundred to eighty doesn't mean you've stopped speeding.*

Here's the call. Let's find rest in the grace of God, power down our overwhelmed mind over the next couple of chapters, and examine what it means to live life under the banner of "It Is Well." When life gets loud, we have to lean close to Jesus and hear His words above the noise. Instead of running around searching for God in our schedules, why don't we stop and listen for a while? Lists are beautiful, but God gave them to keep us in order, not for us to obsess over. The lists God has given us are for our protection, not our entrapment, so don't get so caught up in the rules, that you lose the relationship. In a world that urges us to hold our time, we are held by our Savior. Our freedom to live in Jesus comes from His invitation for more, but not by the world's meaning of "more." For Jesus, finding more was giving it all up for us. We can lay down our weapons and run into His embrace because He's already fought the battle. This book isn't a cute little organized four-step plan. It's an open invitation into the Heart of God because that is where we are free. So, hold on by your bootstraps, or don't. Maybe for once, let your guard down, and let Jesus sweep in. You can find freedom in being held and surrendering the grip on your planner.

Reflection Questions:

1. Let's be honest; do you feel like you're crashing? Journal some words that come to mind when you think about your schedule.

2. Were those words peaceful or stress-related? Sort your words into the categories of peaceful or stress-related.

3. As believers, we have a longing placed in our hearts for more. This was intrinsically designed by the Father to center us back to Him, but when we get off balance, it can be detrimental. We can write anthems, pretty words, or fill our planners, but ultimately, we only find satisfaction in balancing our lives with Jesus. What does a balanced life look like for you?

4. Your challenge for this week is to begin to make that life happen. Whether it's saying no, yes, or pause, start to cultivate with the Holy Spirit what your

Surrender your Planner

What Happens When You Hit the Wall?

In Nascar, vehicles drive insane speeds in order to stay "grounded" and attempt to win the race. We think one hundred miles an hour is flying; they call it a morning warm-up. Races are built on the excitement and propensity for danger at mind-blowing high speeds. The best driver is the one who can win the race without center-punching a wall.

Has your life ever felt like this? Do you gear up every morning for Nascar speeds? You could be battling a difficult job, raising kids, or just simply defeating your own negative self-talk. While the race is different for each of us, we all have one goal: go as fast as you can, get as much done as possible, and win the race.

Sounds like a great plan, correct?

Until, we hit the wall.

It could be we became distracted, overwhelmed, or we were simply just going too fast. But it was bound to happen. The crash could come by way of getting fired, getting sick, or having a breakdown. When it happens to me, I can feel it coming, and my ever-ominous wall moves closer and closer until I finally crash. Coming from someone who has emotionally "crashed" dozens of times in her life, I can tell you, it's not a fun place to be. The realization I've hit the wall is one of the worst because that's when the enemy has a field day with my already-fragile emotions.

Some mornings, I just know I've hit the wall. Other days, it sneaks up on me

The Wild Calling

in a terrifying way.

The wall can actually be the entry point for Jesus, if we allow it. Could you imagine how these Nascar drivers would function if they just blew off their pit crew and went on fixing the car by themselves? Or even worse, if they just started running laps on foot in order to keep up? Unfortunately, this is often the picture we get when something crashes in our life. We push away our pit crew, jump back in the car, and start trying to limp to the finish line just to say we did it.

Here's an idea.

Let's get out of the driver's seat. As simple as this sounds, we have a lot of work to do. Letting go of pride, fear, and control will save us from a lot of heartache, but we have to be willing to give them up.

Paul actually talks about people who struggled with pride such as this in Colossians 2. The Colossian church had become disconnected, doing life on their own, and Paul was very clear that God's way wasn't intended to be done in isolation.

> *They have lost connection with the head, from whom the whole body, supported and held together by its ligaments and sinews, grows as God causes it to grow.*
> Colossians 2:19, NIV

The truth is this: we cannot grow apart from the body of Christ. We can't win the race alone. The word for "held" in that verse is the Greek word *kratōn*. This word is used to describe being held by someone or something, holding fast to a particular person. This word is used to describe how we are held together by God and God alone.

Please know this: you are not responsible for holding together your life, your family, or yourself. Your life is orchestrated by God, and it only stays whole through His power-not your own.

SURRENDER YOUR PLANNER

This is the fun part. When we hit the wall, we realize we can't do it on our own anymore. Luckily, we're not stranded because our Heavenly Father is there to take care of us. He invites us to surrender control of the race to Him, to lean back into His arms and let His peace take care of the frenzy in our minds. Jesus never called us to save the world; He just commanded us to tell others He has saved the world. We don't have the power to help people the way Jesus can, so instead of trying to take charge out of the hands of our Savior, spend some time surrendering your thoughts, schedule, and life to Him all over again.

Reflection Questions:

1. Has there been a time in your life where you have "hit the wall?" Take a couple minutes to write down what happened, how you felt, and how you responded.

2. Did you feel like you had to jump right back up and scramble for peace?

3. When you talk about your life, what are some common phrases you use? It could be something similar to these:
   "Everything is great! I'm just really busy with..."
   "I love all I do! My schedule is slammed..."
   "I wish I could help! I've just got a lot going on, but I'll move some things around and see what I can do."

4. Spend the next week listening to yourself. How do you talk about your life to yourself? Write down the ways you describe this time of life.

5. Spend some time this week being completely still. See what God says when you actually can hear Him.

CHAPTER **8**

LET'S STOP THE FIRE TRUCK

Now that we have talked through our self-reliance and dependency on our schedules, let's talk about freedom. We aren't going to clean our hearts ourselves; that doesn't lead to lasting change. It's time to let Jesus scrub away the core mess of why we do this to ourselves. So, it's time to be honest.

Do you enjoy all that you're doing? For some, the answer is genuinely, "Yes!" But here's another question to follow that up.

Do others enjoy you when you do all you're doing?

If the people around you would avoid answering that question, chances are that you've ceased to be someone they enjoy walking alongside. The truth is that you've stopped walking with people; instead, you're lapping them at breakneck speeds, catching up to them every week or two.

This does not make us enjoyable people to be around. Instead, it makes us the human equivalent of fire trucks. We're shiny, nice, doing good things, but when people hear us coming full force, they screech into the next lane, road, or any other area, in order to avoid getting run over.

If you're coming home frustrated, be honest with yourself. Are you allowing room for the Holy Spirit to help you walk through the day, or are you a five-alarm fire truck, screeching by the people you're called to do life with?

This is your wake-up call. Long gone are the days where we can get by with shallow, "I'm great!" answers, as we blow by people. For the love of the Lord, and to avoid any other tragedies or corrosive interactions, slow your roll. In fact, text three of your closest friends or loved ones, and ask them these questions:

- Do I appear to enjoy all that I'm doing?
- Am I enjoyable to be around in this stage of life?
- What would you like to see me give up in order to have more free time?

Things like laundry, taking care of a sick loved one, or getting things done around the house are almost non-negotiable. But if those things are too much, ask the Holy Spirit to show you how to ask for help and make your load lighter. If you're overwhelmed at work, set healthy boundaries by having a conversation with your boss and team about workplace expectations. Many times, we take on so much because we believe no one else will do it, but in reality, a lot of the small, time-consuming responsibilities we shoulder throughout the day could be distributed to someone else. If you're the boss, stop picking up stamps when the office runs out. Delegation is the key to sanity, and while it's humbling to ask for help, it can be one place in your life where you find freedom to breathe. Look for ways you can serve and show the love of Christ to your office, your family, or your church without completely draining your soul.

Reflection Questions:

1. Take a minute and think about the question, "Do you enjoy all you're doing?" Write down what comes to mind if you were to respond to that question.

2. Take a moment, and imagine if someone re-iterated the above statements to you. Do they sound genuine? Or do they sound pre-rehearsed or planned?

3. Ask yourself what people would say about you if they were asked whether or not you are enjoyable to be around. You could be very well-intentioned with the heart behind your motives, but if you are burnt out, worn down, or harsh with others, your schedule could be an emotional blind spot.

4. Vulnerability is scary; isn't it? I think the opportunities to ask hard questions are gifts from God, but other people might not feel that way. If you have had an emotional blind spot towards people in this place in your life, pray that the Lord gives you opportunities to be bold and to open up and ask for forgiveness. The first step to change is the bravery to start, and this could be your starting place, dear friend.

5. Schedule one meeting this week, whether it's a phone call or a face-to-face meeting, to sit down with someone close to you and ask them the question, "Am I enjoyable to be around at this moment?" Pray the Lord will soften your heart towards their answer, whatever it is, and that you'll have ears to receive.

The Wild Calling

Finally, Let's Take A Nap

You can only be held when you surrender what's in your hands.

I don't know if you have ever babysat or if you have children of your own, but children happen to be my favorite example when it comes to surrender.

Several years ago, I babysat for the child of friends who reminded me so much of myself; it was terrifying. I watched this child fight sleep, ignore siblings, and push everyone away, to get a certain LEGO set built. When it finally came time for the kids to go to bed, she stiffened, locking up her little legs, and refusing to be carried to bed. She became dead-weight like a board in my arms. I finally coaxed her to her room under the guise she didn't have to go to sleep; she just had to sit on her bed. That was pretty genius in my mind!

Once we finished getting ready for bed, she crawled onto the bed and loudly announced she was staying up all night, crossing her arms across her chest. I said goodnight, giggling as I walked back down the stairs because I knew what was going to happen.

Five minutes later, this stubborn child was fast asleep, still in the upright position they had so staunchly taken.

How many times do we do this with the Lord? We push everyone away in order to get our projects accomplished, our schedules filled, and our people-pleasing criteria met for the week. When God finally calls us to surrender, we act no better than a small child. We pout, stiffen up, and bargain with God to try to get what we want. Ultimately, He isn't trying to call us to something that will be

LET'S STOP THE FIRE TRUCK

harmful to us, but rather, He's inviting us to rest. When we finally surrender, we can instantly assume a position of real rest.

What's something God is calling you to rest from that you are deliberately pushing against?

It could be work, a friendship, a relationship, or even a sin or insecurity. God isn't calling you to rest to hurt you, and newsflash: the world will function just fine if you say "no" every once in a while.

A daily practice of resting in the Father's arms is how we are going to find true surrender. Resting in the Father's arms doesn't have to be a big, long ceremony. We have Jesus, who, by His sacrifice, allows us to run straight to God's arms and jump in His lap.

We can rest in His presence driving the kids to school, getting up a few minutes earlier or staying up a few minutes later to read the Bible and journal, or by going for a run with some friends. There's no limit to what God says we can and can not do for rest in His presence, minus one thing: we cannot find true rest if we are coming at it as an item on the to-do list. We'll get something accomplished and maybe hear some encouragement from His Word, but if we do it to get it done, we'll stay in a position of anxious striving.

> *"Come to me, all you who are weary and burdened, and I will give you rest. Take my yoke upon you and learn from me, for I am gentle and humble in heart, and you will find rest for your souls. For my yoke is easy and my burden is light."*
> Matthew 11:28-30, NIV

Reflection Questions:

1. What is something you find keeps you from resting in God's presence?

2. The next time you sit down with your Bible, observe how you go about spending time with the Lord. Do you do it from a place of accomplishment or from a position of childlike curiosity, eager to learn more about your Heavenly Father?

3. Are you stiffening up in an area of your life? It could be a sin, a relationship, or something God has commanded you to do that is scary for you. Breathe deep, sit in His presence, and ask Him.

4. What's one thing the Lord is calling you to act upon in this season of life that you've been running from? It could be starting back to church, quitting a job, or even just getting to bed a bit earlier.

5. How are you going to practically rest in God's presence in the coming weeks? Write out an action plan, and tape it to your mirror, your fridge, or put it in your phone! Spiritual habits only form with consistency.

Chapter 9

Rest for the Weary

"One more rep!" My trainer screamed from the sidelines, while I was hunched over next to a tire, pouring sweat and breathing harder than I ever had before. I thought this workout was going to be the end of me. I was exhausted. I had given it everything I had, and I was out of steam. There was a lot more going on in this scene, and the average person wasn't able to see my internal struggle.

I had spent the last fifty-five minutes shaming and hating my body. I had called myself every name possible, thought about the way I looked in the mirror, and merged that with my failure to complete the exercise on the field. I was gross and disgusting, and I felt so alone. I had started working out to lose weight, as I was about sixty-five pounds "too heavy," in my opinion. Years of emotional eating had landed me into a pattern of constant body shaming. Instead of fixing my heart and realizing *I was fearfully and wonderfully made*, I had shut down and shut out the people around me when it came to being confident in my body. Instead, I found myself battling my mind and Satan's lies on a turf field, and the lies were winning. I was alone in the world, or so I thought. I hung my head for the last time and decided to quit. Then, I heard it.

The cheering.

People were shouting for me. They were encouraging *me* to keep going.

The Wild Calling

I had written off finishing well, allowed the enemy to win, and was ready to give up.

But then I heard them.

People in the class had noticed my struggle and had stopped their own workouts to cheer me on. Trainers, athletes, and folks just like me were encouraging me to just keep going. While this single act of cheering me on to completion didn't win the mental battle, it did chip away at the darkness. When I realized people around me genuinely saw me for who I was and helped me feel less alone, I could complete the task before me. Looking back on this stage of life, I was reminded of Exodus 17, when the Israelites went to battle with the Amalekites. When Moses raised his hands, the Israelites started winning, but when he got tired and lowered his hands, the Amalekites started to take the victory.

As long as Moses held up his hands, Israel prevailed; but when he lowered them, Amalek prevailed. When Moses' hands grew heavy, they took a stone and put it under him, and he sat on it. Then Aaron and Hur held his hands up, one on each side, so that his hands remained steady until the sun went down.
Exodus 17:11-12, BSB

When I got tired, my friends in the gym cheered me on, and I was able to win the battle in my mind by completing the workout. When life gets hard and things happen that are too much to handle on your own, look for the people around you to hold your arms up. Jesus does not call us to do life alone, and our friends can help us win battles that we could never conquer otherwise. Community is God-given, ordained, and blessed when we keep Him at the center and help each other fight our battles. If you're weary today, ask someone to hold your arms up in this battle, and be looking for others who need you to remind them they can defeat the enemy.

REST FOR THE WEARY

Reflection Questions:

1. Can you list the people in your life that are lifting your arms when you get tired?

2. In what ways can you seek Jesus even when you're weary?

3. If you're doing life alone, I encourage you to reach out to someone and ask for a time when you can meet. Community has to be built. What's one step you can take towards that today?

Juice Cleanses and Jesus

*Thus the heavens and the earth were completed in all their vast array.
By the seventh day God had finished the work he had been doing;
so on the seventh day he rested from all his work. Then God blessed
the seventh day and made it holy, because on it he rested
from all the work of creating that he had done.*
Genesis 1:1-3, NIV

Just in case you've missed the latest trend, self-care is currently marketed as the best form of therapy. We've all seen the curated "rest" days filled with pedicures and yummy brunches, but let's be honest, when rest is treated like an itinerary to accomplish things instead of scheduling time to soak in the Father's presence, it is no longer the rest God intended. We are called to intentionally seek out rest in our Heavenly Father's presence, not shut out the world to get extra things on our to-do list accomplished.

I struggle with this quite frequently, and I have realized I am not doing myself or my relationship with Jesus any good if I am isolating myself from the community in order to binge-watch my favorite TV show. I had to open up to friends and trusted spiritual leaders about my tendency to retreat from everyone (including the Lord) when I become overwhelmed and frustrated. It's taken a while to cultivate change in this area, but when I spend time with the Lord, resting in His presence, I crave returning to it as soon as possible.

This is not another one of those "treat-yo-self" speeches, but a reminder that rest is commanded by our Heavenly Father. While they are helpful, a facial and a massage aren't the cure-alls to heart problems. We can have days full of self-care, but when "self" is our focus, we can't fill ourselves back up. The only way we are refreshed is through the power of the Holy Spirit. One of the things I'm discovering is rest isn't just our body's natural craving, it's also a desire of our hearts.

We were created and modeled after a Creator God who rested on the seventh day, encouraged time alone in periods of refuge for King David, and even called His own Son to rest away from His busy schedule of ministering to others. When we rest, we not only create a space in which to be more like Jesus, we actually end up with more capacity to treat others the way He has called us to treat them. When our souls make their home in Jesus, we find rest. He has given us a capacity for accomplishing great things, but He has also tied our spiritual and physical health to the amount of time we rest with Him.

Trying to get it all done in a day of rest will just leave you as weary as your other days. The thing about doing it all is you can't do it all *well*. As a college student, I worked full time, went to school, had multiple hobbies or side hustles, and tried to have a social life. If you're in college now, you know that I was just about worn to the point of breaking down. If you're not in college yet, take heed and don't overwhelm your schedule to the level I did. As Christians, we believe taking on a lot of good things makes us more like Jesus, but in all honesty, it just makes us really tired. You don't have to move lightning-fast in order to move forward; instead, use this time to figure out what God has for you and learn His voice.

If you are broken down, weary, and tired of faking it, just pause. When God plants us in a spot, we can't grow faster than we're supposed to grow. As children of a Heavenly Father who wants good things for us, we are made to thrive. Just like a well-tended garden, we are supposed to bloom from a place of nourishment and security. Our Abba didn't create us to live out of a striving for man's approval; He made us for His glory, and He is glorified when we fill our souls with Him.

Rest has always been something I've resented. I don't like to take time for myself because I can always think of ten things I should be doing instead. As I've walked through different times, I've watched myself resent rest in different

ways. I've self-loathed on my days off, I've guilt-tripped others into working when we should have been relaxing, and I've just outright refused to participate in God's beckoning for me to rest. I was wrapped up in the concept I wasn't being a good enough Christian when I was being still and resting in God. Christians are movers and shakers of culture, or so I told myself. So, when I attached my worth to every activity I did instead of attaching it to the Creator, I shortchanged myself on the adventure of following my wild calling. The truth is I can be a great mover and shaker for the Kingdom when I'm firmly rooted in Christ and nothing else.

Seasons of waiting are not supposed to be idle stages. When we feel dismal about our wait, we must remember where we started. We've been intentionally placed in Christ, and we root our identities in Him. This truth makes rest feel like an extension of our calling, not something we have to push away. I've learned God often reveals Himself most powerfully in periods of rest, when we are the quietest.

One year, after college, the world got loud, and my brain became even louder. My anxious thoughts shouted at me like there was a megaphone in my head, and the only solution was to outrun the panicked thoughts or to become completely still. In that period of stress, I developed the mindset I didn't deserve rest because I hadn't done anything to earn it. This led to an inevitable breakdown, which would have been avoidable had I just rested in the first place.

Not only did I push away rest like it was the plague, I cut out people who reminded me that rest was a command from God. I bought into the "hustle culture" and found myself extremely worn out. Somehow though, being busy felt safer than confronting the fact I was miserable. I hated school, was overworked, and was truly unhappy with who I was becoming. I frantically journaled one night, "In the moments when the noise fades, does joy remain?" In my term of unholy hustle, the answer was no. I had no rest, and underneath that, I had no joy. Rest isn't something we buy into when we have a couple of days off from work; it's a position our hearts desperately seek. If God is my priority, I won't find myself frayed and worn with the vacuum of the world.

One of the best ways to rest is to find spiritual rest. It's not sitting around and napping all day but intentionally allowing the Lord to heal places in your heart that hurt you. You can find spiritual rest in showing mercy.

I was sitting at Starbucks with a lukewarm coffee, and I was frustrated. This early Monday morning appointment had been on my calendar for weeks, and the friend I was supposed to meet was running 20 minutes late. She hadn't texted me, and I was starting to get incredibly annoyed. *She knows my time is valuable, just like hers. Why wouldn't she text me if she was going to be this late!?!* The narrative of ungracious thoughts continued until about ten minutes later when she texted me. She had been at another Starbucks waiting on me. I realized, when I checked my phone, I was the one who was late because I had gone to the wrong spot! I instantly hopped in my car and found myself becoming the most merciful person *to myself*. The conviction I felt for being so unfair was overwhelming. She was more than kind about it, and we look back and laugh to this day.

Has someone ever consumed your thoughts because they've done you wrong? For the 30 minutes I felt wronged at Starbucks, all I could think was a cycle of ungracious thoughts.

If I'm honest, I'm one of those people that struggles with a fierce dislike of someone because I've deemed them "not worthy" of my mercy. They could have offended me, directly or indirectly, or done something unjust. I'm not an easily angered person, but I'll carry grievances in my heart around until they almost eat me alive.

Rest is something I've begun to define as self-mercy. Showing mercy to others is a graciousness to love them however they need, whether they deserve it or not, so the same definition is true for ourselves. Mercy looks unattainable until you determine you are in need of it.

As a follower of Jesus, I'm quick to label myself as merciful and gracious, but when I'm confronted with circumstances that ask me to pull from that belief of extending kindness to everyone, I'm the last to want to volunteer mercy and grace. This pride places my soul in a constant state of torment because I've bought into the grace God has shown me, but I'm refusing to share that grace with others or even myself. I feel ten pounds lighter when I allow the Lord to clean out the hurts I carry around in my spirit.

Psalm 28:6-9 has been a prayer of mine for a while now, but I'm nowhere near perfect.

> *Blessed be the LORD!*
> *For he has heard the voice of my pleas for mercy.*
> *The LORD is my strength and my shield;*
> *in him my heart trusts, and I am helped;*
> *my heart exults,*
> *and with my song I give thanks to him.*
> *The LORD is the strength of his people;*
> *He is the saving refuge of his anointed.*
> *Oh, save your people and bless your heritage!*
> *Be their shepherd and carry them forever.*
> Psalm 28:6-9, ESV

What a beautiful prayer, right? I'm asking God to show me mercy, and out of His mercy, I am called to show it as well. The psalmist (possibly David) says the Lord heard his pleas for mercy, and because he was heard, he'd praise God forever. When the Lord takes us out of something painful and starts to give us spiritual rest, we start to feel a peace that only comes from Him. It could come from removing us from a difficult situation or by commanding us to make some lifestyle changes.

One of the easiest ways I can get some spiritual rest is by setting boundaries. One way I do that is through filtering my social media. I wish I had figured this out in college when Instagram devoured my days, and I was obsessed with displaying a perfect life on social media. When I was a freshman at a large university, I snuck onto the football field to get a great Instagram photo for all my friends to see. The comments of, "I'm so jealous!" or "I wish I did that!" fueled my obsession, regardless of the fact that my soul was empty, and I was scrambling for belonging instead of finding it in Jesus.

I find myself being less merciful with myself or others and also shortchanging my rest to compete with strangers on the Internet. This doesn't mean only follow people if they worship the ground you walk on or constantly tell you how great you are, but choose your social media and online influences wisely. If you follow people who make you angry or who you secretly criticize, do yourself a favor and mute, block, or unfriend them. If you are constantly going to be tearing others down from behind your screen, remove their influence from your life, and ask the Lord what other steps you need to take to redeem and rest your soul. If someone has vastly offended you, maybe even ask them to coffee or lunch, and hash out the issue in a respectful way. If someone is an emotional vampire in your life, set healthy boundaries with them, and keep your distance.

The best way you'll regain a soul at rest is by setting great boundaries with the things that consume you. You can't live in a time of overflow, health, happiness, and rest if you're going to allow small offenses to have such great power over your days. Friends, my soul is tired of empty, polished lives instead of real, joyful living. I'm exhausted for the girls who think they have to get two hundred likes on a selfie to make them worthy.

The goodness of God has nothing to do with the opinion of man, and I want nothing more than to impress that upon each of your hearts. If we could figure this out sooner, rather than later, we would be able to run towards our calling without fear of what others think of us. My encouragement to you is to take some time this week cleaning out the items or people that affect your ability to show and receive mercy and rest. How are you being influenced on an everyday basis, and how can you improve that? If your relationships with others don't draw you closer to God, then ask Him for the peace to make changes for the better.

Reflection Questions:

1. How are you intentionally protecting your spiritual health?

2. Do you feel like other people have a negative influence on your life? In what ways?

3. If you could change your opinion about one person you interact with, how would you change it? Why?

4. Do you think God is calling you to reconcile with someone in your path? How so?

5. Do you feel you are seeking the Lord when it comes to the people you allow to give their opinion in your life?

CHAPTER **10**

WORK AS WORSHIP

It's 6 a.m. Your alarm blares in the background, and you slam the button until it's quiet. It's Monday, and you can already feel the dread of going back to work. Whether it's your boss, your snarky co-worker, or just the simple fact you can't stand your job, Monday is hard for you. You spend the week counting down the hours until 5 p.m., wishing you could pursue your passions, dreams, or career goals. I've been there, and the danger is, it all looks so appealing on the surface. Maybe you have traded your calling for a cushy office job, or maybe God is calling you to lead, and you'd just rather stay in the shadows.

If this is you, it doesn't have to be this way. We were created for worship, and our work is an extension of it. Instead of begrudging our jobs, we should look up to our Heavenly Father and find the abundant life that awaits us. Paycheck to paycheck doesn't have to be a financial term. It could also be an emotional or mental term in our lives. We are hanging on by a thread until the end of the work week. If you daydream about your days off more than you dream about the goodness of God in your work environment, there's a pretty big chance your work isn't an act of worship.

> *Work willingly at whatever you do, as though you were working for the Lord rather than for people.*
> Colossians 3:23, NLT

I'm sure we've all either heard this verse, seen it on Pinterest, or even plastered it on a coffee mug. It's not just a commandment; it's a promise. For me, it began as a begrudging command from the Lord that produced a big impact on my life when I finally obeyed it. My life is a little hectic; I work full time as a realtor, and it's not a job with set hours. I've shown fourteen homes on a Saturday, written contracts from backstage at a worship night, and used to ruin many a family dinner with a "quick" phone call. When our work becomes our idol instead of an act of worship, it starts getting blown out of proportion.

The Dolly Parton song "9-5" is one of my favorite workplace songs. When she talks about pouring herself a cup of ambition, I giggle when I realize that's the best name for coffee I've ever heard. I also think about what it would mean if I started my day with a cup of heavenly ambition and how it would impact my work environment. My job would no longer feel like work. Rather, when filtered through the Holy Spirit, it would be an ambitious act of worship and a sweet offering before the Lord. In order to do this, we have to start looking at our jobs as opportunities to see God's promises revealed, instead of something else to get done before we can get to "church" stuff.

When Colossians 3:23 becomes our promise instead of a task, we start living free from other people's expectations. When we work for the Lord, we find ourselves feeling lighter, more free, and even enjoying work at times. Working for the Lord means we stop living based for accomplishments and instead live out of His abundance.

Abundance isn't born out of accomplishments. Abundance is born out of abiding.

How much stress and worry fill your work days because you're so concerned over the things crowding your to-do list? This isn't abundant living and, deep down, you know it.

Does your stomach hurt and your heart race before work? Do you obsessively rewrite your to-do lists throughout the day so you can watch them get smaller?

Do you put off spending quality time with your family to "get more done"?

Abundance doesn't mean stressful striving. Set the to-do list down, and start breathing in the life-giving air of God's promises. He's the Creator of the universe, and He's got you covered, even at work.

Reflection Questions:

1. What is your favorite thing about your job?

2. What is your least favorite thing about your job?

3. What is your response to stress at your job? How do you cope when things get hard?

4. If you could do anything in the world, what would you do? What's holding you back from that?

My challenge to you is to write Colossians 3:23, on a notecard, and tape it to your workspace, or set a reminder on your phone to read it at least a couple of times a day. Look at it as a promise, not an order. God isn't adding another thing to your plate; He's trying to remind you, He holds the plate. We weren't created to hold it all together.

Holy Hustle

When our work is an act of worship, the people we are around start to notice a difference. Marketing, social media, and business have all led to two types of influences: ones that manipulate or inspire. Human nature is all about finding someone to follow or something to work towards, whether out of fear or out of love. When it comes to our work being worship, we need to treat everyone with the same respect and kindness Christ has shown to us. Whether you're an intern or a CEO, your role has weight and value in the Kingdom.

Culture has given us the impression we have to be hardcore to be good at our jobs. With shows like *Empire* and *Dynasty,* women, both in the workplace and at home, are championed for being brittle or cold. This culture has led to a disconnect between people and has even been listed as one of the main reasons people leave their jobs. When the word "boss" is associated with an explicative addition, we defy the intricacies of God assigning us roles and defer to earthly pressure for power. Calling people things such as "hardcore," "bossy," or "control-freak," doesn't advance the Kingdom, and when we use these terms on our fellow sisters, we discourage them in their wild calling and can defeat their motivation.

When worship becomes a competition, God isn't glorified by the hustle.

Yes, we are called to pursue excellence, but we answer to something other than our time card. If the hardened hustle is wearing you out, take off the mask of having it all together. Show that you can let your walls down and invite someone along for the ride. God is glorified when we stop competing in the race He's already won. When I stop competing with others, He can be glorified in work, and that's where my hustle becomes holy.

Reflection Questions:

1. Do you feel what you do at work glorifies God? In what ways?

2. In what ways do you feel like you can come alongside your co-workers and build them up?

3. What are some practical ways you can stop hustling out of striving and start working from who God says you are called to be?

Hustling Alone Isn't the Answer

Pretending you're perfect not only hurts you in your workplace, but it actually isolates you from your coworkers. Being the girl that has her life "Pinterest-perfect" means you can also be incredibly intimidating to the people around you. How many times do you crave someone who will lock arms with you, and say, *"Girl, I'm exactly where you are, and it's really hard."*

If you crave this in your workplace, be that person to someone else! I had co-workers at previous jobs who I intentionally sought out to encourage each day. Whether it was a compliment or an offer to pick up lunch for them, I could shift the atmosphere at work by allowing God's love to shine through me to others. Asking for help is another thing I struggled with, so now I try to surround myself with people who are better at my job than I am! It makes the workload a lot more fun because we aren't competing with one another, and God gets the glory from our hard work and my humility.

Just because it's hard to admit you're not perfect doesn't mean God is any less glorified. 1 John 1:8-10 makes this point by saying,

> *If we claim that we're free of sin, we're only fooling ourselves. A claim like that is errant nonsense. On the other hand, if we admit our sins—make a clean breast of them—he won't let us down; he'll be true to himself. He'll forgive our sins and purge us of all wrongdoing. If we claim that we've never sinned, we out-and-out contradict God—make a liar out of him. A claim like that only shows off our ignorance of God.*
> 1 John 1:8-10, MSG

We were created in His image, not as carbon copies of Him. We will mess up, make mistakes, and be beautifully human. This is what makes us who we are: perfectly imperfect and *fearfully and wonderfully made*. God gets the glory when you are open and real, but the enemy does not want to see that type of freedom exist. You are your harshest critic, and the enemy uses this to cripple and isolate you in your workplace. Open wide the doors of your life and be honest, and you might just find yourself loving what you do even more.

> *Remember that the Lord will give you an inheritance as your reward, and that the Master you are serving is Christ.*
> Colossians 3:24, NLT

WORK AS WORSHIP

Whether you are at home, in the workplace, at church, or volunteering, you are not striving for man's approval. God is the only one who gives praise that matters or has eternal weight. The call to be open and real might be wild and scary. Please know there is so much joy to be found in the middle of the mundane, and you might just find that you really love where you work.

Reflection Questions:

1. What is your biggest motivation to do your job well?

2. Do you feel like your co-workers judge you? How?

3. What scares you the most about being vulnerable at work?

4. Do you work out of motivation or out of fear? Can you tell the difference between the two?

5. What's one way you can view your work as an act of worship this week?

CHAPTER **11**

The Brick Wall

Okay; let's be honest. How burnt out do you feel when it comes to your job? If you answered with a resounding sigh, there's more than a slight chance you've hit your brick wall.

Walls can be good. In the Old Testament, Rahab was an unlikely woman God used in spite of the walls that existed around her. Rahab's issue was twofold; she was a prostitute, and she was helping the Israelite spies. Her work was one that was shamed in culture and especially by God's people.

> *"Our lives for your lives!" the men assured her. "If you don't tell what we are doing, we will treat you kindly and faithfully when the Lord gives us the land."*
> Joshua 2:14, NIV

Rahab saw past her job title to her calling, and she ended up saving the two Israelite spies. In turn, God saved her family from harm. In today's world, looking past your title or social opinions can mean the difference between playing it safe and choosing abundant living.

When was the last time you saw beyond your job title to a Kingdom goal?

When we are feeling burnt out, it's hard for us to see our callings, even when

The Wild Calling

they're right in front of us. We start making it about working hard, hustling, or getting a paycheck. This leads to us looking down at our own two feet instead of looking around for the opportunities God puts in our paths.

The truth of feeling burnt out is this: when our hustle is no longer about Jesus and all about us, we can find that the walls close in, and we start getting overwhelmed. I find myself getting the most overwhelmed when I've spent too much time by myself, focused on what I need to get done instead of what God is doing around me.

When you feel like the world is closing in around you, just look up. Grab coffee with a friend, walk the dog, or drive around listening to a podcast or worship music. All these things can help you stop focusing down the narrow tunnel of your work and instead on what God has set out for you to do for the Kingdom.

Don't neglect your job by any means, but stay alert to what God is doing around you. You might not be hiding spies, but you could be loving on a co-worker or ministering to a friend.

The truth is this: God uses walls not to trap us but to help us focus our eyes upward to what He is doing.

Reflection Questions:

1. Do you feel trapped in what you do?

2. What takes a lot of your focus at work?

3. If you could focus on loving one person this week, who would it be?

4. How would you like to be intentionally cared for in this stage of life?

5. What's one area of your job you'd like to focus on in order to make it an act of worship this week?

Abundance is Scary

Are we really excited to live abundantly, or are we afraid of finally seeing God made real in our lives? I had a friend gracious enough to drag me to this realization in the parking lot of a Starbucks one day. She reminded me I could either live in a place of abundance or keep working out the plans for my life on my own terms, which would lead to burn out and exhaustion. If I'm honest, abundance is scary. It's terrifying to realize God's kingdom is becoming fully alive and evident in your everyday life. It means your small, human-sized dreams have been taken up into the hands of your Heavenly Father, and He's molded

The Wild Calling

them into something so beautiful. For some reason, that terrifies me to no end.

It's fun to watch Him build, but are we willing to lay down our small tools in order to step aside as He creates something beautiful? That's the difference between accomplishing and abiding. When we lay down our own creations to watch the Creator work, we can watch Him take our small-scale dreams and make them fully alive. Our accomplishments pale in comparison to His magnificent plan. I think the Creator of our heart is writing a story so much bigger than our next business idea or marketing plan. Trusting that story is the heart of abundant living.

"What next?" That's the question I found myself asking as I went to quit my comfy corporate job to take up freelance work. I'd like to say it was a neat faith story, where I held God's hand, and He guided me to some amazing things.

I am not that cute, and real-life isn't that neat.

I remember crying at my desk, on my lunch break, and to my friends and family about how hard that stage felt. I took the job because I didn't want to freelance full-time, even though that's what God had directly called me to at the time. I ran to a steady paycheck over the word of God, and I regretted it. Much like the Israelites, I picked up my pack and started on my forty-year journey in circles. It was one of the most painful things I've ever experienced, but it did serve a purpose. I learned how to best serve the Kingdom, and that is by laying down my pride and picking up my calling. What my nine-to-five job did was teach me how to settle and be complacent in a financially safe environment, and it taught me what abundant living did not look like.

I found the most significant confirmations to ministry, freelance, and so many other things when I took God my comfy little nine-to-five job and laid it at His feet.

My life has Kingdom value, so why would I ever sacrifice so much time fulfilling an agenda created out of fear?

Here's what followed.

The Brick Wall

My work is now an act of worship, and it is one of the most obvious places I find abundant living. I have an amazing career that I wake up every day excited about, have incredible ministry opportunities, and I get to watch God build my faith through my surrender.

Reflection Questions:

1. What's next? How is your work an act of worship?

2. What's your next step to abundant living?

3. Take some time to write your abundant life goals below.

CHAPTER **12**

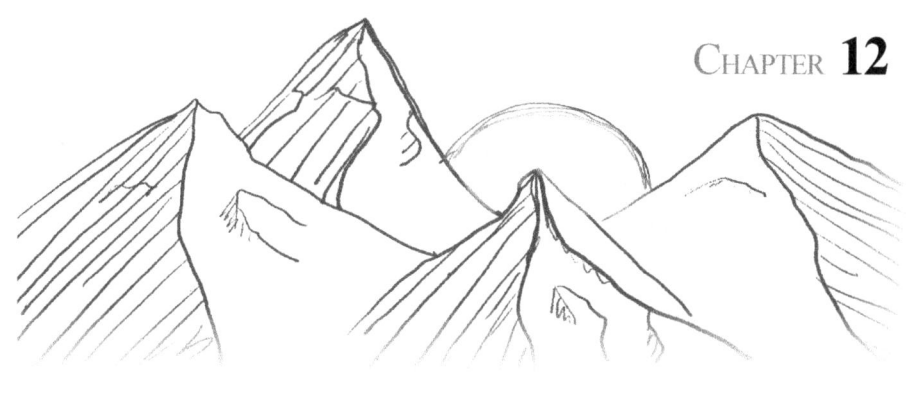

BRAVERY IN HARD AND HOLY SPACES

I've recently been singing a line in a song that talks about raising a hallelujah, even in the midst of our enemies. This verse has been repeated a million times during worship on Sunday mornings and throughout the week, but I had never really thought through the words. Singing praises in front of people I would consider my enemies would be something I couldn't imagine doing. I was working on beautiful things in ministry and seeing God redeem. I raised a hallelujah, but I didn't know enemies were around me.

Realizing someone wasn't looking out for my best interest is one of the most humbling things I've ever experienced. "In the presence of my enemies" has been my experience in meeting rooms when I've watched my ideas for growth get shot down because they made someone uncomfortable. "In the presence of my enemies" has been my experience leading worship on stages where I was told I didn't belong or wasn't fitting in. "In the presence of my enemies" has been my experience in friendships where I've opened my whole heart to someone and then watched as they dismissed my vulnerability because of their insecurities. "In the presence of my enemies" has been my experience while fighting for a seat at the table where I never thought I would belong. "In the presence of my enemies" has been in times where I've been told I am not enough.

Now, don't get me wrong. People did not set out to be my enemies. A lot of times, we try to make people the bad guy, where, in all reality, Satan is the one who is actively working to destroy our dreams and crush our callings. People we would call our enemies are not necessarily setting out to become our enemies, but Satan can use their insecurities and woundings to wound and harm us. As Christians, we can even become enemies to one another when we push our own agenda instead of the gospel.

But there's always hope.

The song doesn't talk about running away from our enemies in order to sing our praises, but rather, we are called to sing our praises when we're face-to-face with the people who have hurt us. When the enemy sends things our way, one of the biggest testimonies we can have is raising praise right back to his face.

When God tested Abraham and asked him to sacrifice Isaac, it took him by surprise. Here was God's good and perfect gift, and now he was being asked to give it up. Instead of running away from the sacrifice, he offered his son, and God rewarded Abraham's obedience. Isaac went on to fulfill the promises God had for His people, and in times when we question raising a hallelujah, Genesis 22, is a point of reference to keep going.

Abraham says to God, *"Here I am,"* and God responds by providing a sacrifice in the form of a ram. The Bible doesn't record whether or not Abraham argued with God, questioned His goodness or His motives, but it does record that he did everything the Lord asked him to do, even when he didn't understand it. What started out looking like a reckless sacrifice to man, ended up being an example of God's unfailing provision.

Even in the hard spaces, we can be reckless in our obedience, when we are confident in God's abundance.

Reflection Questions:

1. Where are you called to raise a hallelujah in your life?

2. In what areas do you see God's abundance today?

3. In what places in your life do you think you are "in the presence of enemies"?

Holy Space

"Your faith has made you well."
Luke 17:19b, NIV

Have you ever been in the season of life where everything is going great, and that kind of freaks you out? If you have, this might be something for you. If you haven't, hopefully, it will help you in the future. I've spent a good portion of the past couple of months in a weird stage of holy space. It's hustling for purpose disguised as busyness, but not in a soul-exhausting way. You might find yourself in this stage if you are:
- content with work
- relationships are going well
- serving in the church and loving it
- coming out of a big occasion in your life and finally enjoying rest

If you're nodding your head *yes* to any of these, welcome, my friend, to holy space. My definition of it is: The place where the courage to say *yes* meets the surrender to look into the heart of God and ask, "What's next?" and then following His answer rather than trying to take the reins.

If this is your season, it's a beautiful one. If you're just barely holding on to your purpose, this study is still for you. Starting this journey into holy space is going to be a wild ride, dear one. Just hold on! We have to have faith in order to enter into the holy spaces God calls us to, the ones where we find healing and freedom. When I think of holy spaces to look to for an illustration, I think of a couple of different examples found in the Bible. These patterns will help us connect the Holy Space and how to identify it in our own lives.

When we read Mark 5:21-43, we can see there are two healings that take place: the woman with the blood disorder and Jairus' daughter who had died. The similarities in these two healings should not be missed. The faith of these individuals should not be overlooked. The woman with the blood disorder knew Jesus was enough for her, and her faith made her well. While Jairus had to overcome the death of his daughter, he knew God was calling him to a holy space where miracles would happen. Healing is found in the holy space where we can ask for help. God used their pain to draw them into a holy space with Him, and He used their healing to show them His heart. He healed both of these people so they could live out their wild calling for His glory.

For twelve years, the woman had suffered an illness. Jairus had watched his daughter grow for twelve years without any sign of illness or blemish. Both were confronted with a period of pain, and when they were, it became very evident healing was their first priority. For the woman with the bleeding disorder, there was a visible and daily reminder that she was unwell. When Jairus' daughter passed away, his pain was physical and also consumed his heart completely.

When illness happens, where do you turn? It could be physical, emotional, spiritual, or mental illness, but when the trial starts, it can be easy to look for coping mechanisms. Some people throw themselves into work, school, friends, or even unhealthy methods such as excessive drinking or other vices. Ultimately, holy space is found when we can lay all else aside and ask for help. If everything is going well, search the hidden places of your heart, and ask the Lord if there's something you need to grow in to prepare you for the times to come.

I've been asking the Lord to make me a cheerful homekeeper. I know that's not normally something people need growth in, but I struggle with the concept that if I'm the only one who deals with it, I don't need to worry about keeping the house neat. Currently, I'm sharing my abode with two pups, and while they complain when I don't let them chase squirrels, they're not exactly going to mind if I don't make my bed every morning. I've never valued a well-kept home, but through time with the Lord, I started to think through why. I am terribly insecure when it comes to hosting people. I genuinely freak out that my house won't be good enough, clean enough, or have nice enough stuff. This makes it easier for me to isolate myself from others and never have people over in the first place.

What the Lord has revealed to me in this stage of digging deep is I don't feel like my house is enough for others to share in because I feel like I'm not good enough to host them. When I use my home as a space for selfishness, God isn't glorified, but when I use it to love others, using the gifts of hospitality He asked me to grow, He is glorified. My wild calling in this season is to grow the gifts I've been reluctant to use and let people use my home as a place to further fall in love with Jesus. There are so many tangible ways to do that, like hosting a Bible study, offering a home as a place where a weary friend can rest, or even allowing someone to store their things in the garage when they're moving and between places to live.

Reflection Questions

1. Where is an area in your life where you feel the need for healing?

2. When something bad happens, what is your coping mechanism?

3. What keeps you from asking for help in the bad periods of life?

4. Why do you think the Lord hasn't healed a particularly painful area in your life yet?

5. Do you have a friend who desperately needs some support in her healing? If so, give her a call today. Grab some coffee, and sit with her in faith, praying confidence over her that the Lord will do what He's promised.

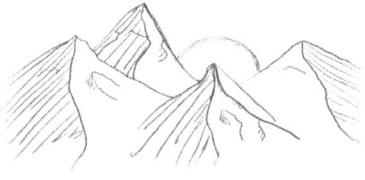

When tragic circumstances arise, look for Jesus.

In Mark 5, the woman with the blood disorder searched for answers when pain hit. Medicine failed her, but as she searched for physicians that would heal her, God was making a way for her path to cross with the Messiah. During those twelve years, I cannot imagine the questioning and heartbreak that took place. She probably, like many of us, began to wonder about her place in the world and God's plan for her in it. The hemorrhaging may have caused her to doubt her worth when society had cast her aside, to doubt her place in the world, and so much more. But God never forgot her.

Sometimes, the only thing stopping us from healing is our inability to accept the invitation from Jesus to be healed.

The physicians robbed the woman of more than just her money; they robbed her of her dignity and gave her another diagnosis: shame.

> *"And there was a woman who had had a discharge of blood for twelve years, and though she had spent all her living on physicians, she could not be healed by anyone."*
> Luke 8:43, ESV

But when she heard about Jesus, she believed He could heal her, and it changed her forever. She knew she had been healed the moment she discreetly touched His cloak, but Jesus asked her to step forward. His goal was not to embarrass her. He acknowledged the healing in a crowd of people, and this was a second healing. Jesus healed her blood issue but also healed her shame issue. By saying she was now healed *and* whole, Jesus not only fixed her body but told her she was made new in His eyes.

> *This is how much God loved the world: He gave his Son, his one and only Son. And this is why: so that no one need be destroyed; by believing in him, anyone can have a whole and lasting life. God didn't go to all the trouble of sending his Son merely to point an accusing finger, telling the world how bad it was. He came to help, to put the world right again.*
> *John 3:16, MSG*

Reflection Questions:

1. How is God calling you to live healed and whole?

2. If there is something you are asking God to heal you from, I encourage you to write down some of His promises and pray them over your healing.

3. If you were made new today, what would that change about how you live your life?

CHAPTER 13

SHAME ISSUE

When Jesus says you are supposed to live loved and abundantly, that's your sole identity. Instead of anxious striving, our healing becomes the launching pad to our calling. By believing that she was healed and beloved, the woman with the blood disorder could live a life far beyond the pain that had crippled her for the past twelve years. Jesus not only freed her from pain but freed her for her perceived destiny.

How many of us need this dual healing? For so long, we carry scar tissue from old wounds, whether physical or not. Oftentimes, I think we cope with the offenses of others worse than any other diagnosis. The pain others have caused is far worse than back pain or migraines. There's a soul ache, not just a hurting body. I find freedom when I realize all Jesus wants me to do is find Him in my brokenness and stretch out my hand. That's where healing begins, on the seam of His robe. My encouragement to you today would be this: if you're seeking freedom from pain, stretch out your hand to the Lord. He is waiting to not only free you from pain but to call you towards your wild calling. It's a beautiful journey and is absolutely worth everything you leave behind.

Reflection Questions:

1. Do you feel the wounds caused by others can be just as crippling as

physical ailments? In what ways have you seen that play out in your own life and the lives of others around you?

2. When it comes to pain, the Messiah is more than equipped to heal. What's stopping you from bringing your pain to Him?

3. How do you handle being wounded? What is your instinctive reaction? Is it one that stems from holiness or from past hurts?

4. In the notes section of this chapter, I want you to write a mini-letter to one person who has wounded you in your life. It could be anyone but focus less on the wounding and more on the person. Try to spend some time looking at them through the eyes of Jesus, and pray the Lord heals them from their hurt, and you from yours.

SHAME ISSUE

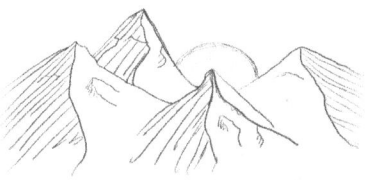

Healing happens when you believe fear has to go

I once read a post from a friend who declared that there are never-ending "stretching" places in our life. As Christians, we like to think that we grow a bit, then rest, then grow, and the cycle goes on and on. Ultimately, we're never out of stretching times. We just stretch in different ways. When we heal, whether it's physical, mental, emotional, or spiritual healing, it can be ground for new purpose and identity, but it can also create pockets of fear in our hearts. When you come out of a hard period, it often feels like a relief, yet a wave of anxiety can sweep in. You may start to question if the hard season is going to come back or when it does, if you'll be prepared for it? Sometimes a devastating crater in our walk with Jesus is actually our greatest invitation to follow Him. Our surrender to the stretching is the first step to embracing our calling to Him.

For me, healing happens when I believe God is in control of the particular stage of my life. In order to begin to heal in a certain area, I have to do a couple of things:

- believe God is who He says He is
- believe His plans are better than mine
- trust His timing is perfect, and mine is flawed
- know my pace is God-ordained; no faster, no slower
- know He isn't going anywhere

If I anchor myself in these five truths, I can open the door for Him to invite me into a holy space, one where He speaks the truth about my season and heals my brokenness.

The thing that stops me from healing 99% of the time is fear. I'm afraid of more

brokenness, I'm afraid God's plans will fail, or I'm afraid I'm going to miss out on something way better. Do you think the woman with the blood disorder had the same fears? That after years of shame and exposure, Jesus was going to shame and expose her for her brokenness as well as her bodily issue? That her discreet search for healing was full of shame and that no one would ever be able to fix her physical illness? And that would cause emotional trauma as well? Dear one, this is never the case with our Savior. Healing starts when we look past fear and lock eyes with Jesus.

Reflection Questions

1. Do you struggle to believe that God is who He says He is regarding your healing, yet you preach that to others effortlessly?

2. Why is it hard to believe God's timing is perfect in your life?

3. What would your life look like right now if it was going at your pace?

4. Step outside of your wants and desires for one moment, and try to see your season from God's perspective. In your opinion, why is He doing what He's doing?

5. Try to take time this week to sit and reflect on the past couple of stages of life you've walked through. Note times when God has been good, faithful, and come through in His abundant way. Hopefully, this will encourage you in this time of life and give you some perspective.

Healing Doesn't have to Make the News

Jairus called his daughter "my dear daughter," and begged Jesus for healing. He asked Jesus for a physical touch. All Jesus needed to heal her was the invitation. Jairus' daughter was more of an exercise in faith than physical healing. When Jesus healed the girl, He commanded that no one should know what had happened in that room. This was a measure of caution for Jairus and his family, largely because if the home were surrounded by gossips, the word of healing would spread quickly. This would cause unnecessary attention to Jairus and his family and distract from the miracle.

> *"They arrived at Jairus' house, where Jesus saw the confusion and heard all the loud crying and wailing. He went in and said to them, "Why all this confusion? Why are you crying? The child is not dead—she is only sleeping!" They started making fun of him, so he put them all out, took the child's father and mother and his three disciples, and went into the room where the child was lying."*
> Mark 5:38-40, GNT

Sometimes, in a holy space, there is just enough room for you, Jesus, and maybe a few close friends. If the town gossips are surrounding your home, it's not because they want to pray over you for healing. Holy space with Jesus pushes out all negatives, even nosy neighbors, and that's exactly how God wants it to be. Healing is found where gossip, speculation, and fear are pushed out. Mark 5:41 (GNT), tells us that Jesus pushes out fear and speaks the following words:

"Talitha cumi" Aramaic meaning, *"Little girl, arise!"*

How many times have we begged God for these words? Life gets hard, we fall down and get discouraged, and then we find ourselves lying face down in the dirt or even dead. Jesus doesn't call us to stay down. He ignites us with words of life. We are His chosen people, and everything else fades away when we claim that as our sole identity. The gossips, naysayers, and town criers in our lives have temporary influences, but are drowned out by Jesus standing over us, speaking, "Little girl, arise!" With those words, Jesus brought healing. He spoke to the woman with the blood, "You're healed and whole," and with those words, He gave a new identity.

We've got both of those promises on our side in this season of holy space. All that's left is to find the Savior, ever waiting and ready to heal us, and ask, "What's next?" There is so much healing to be found in the presence of our Ultimate Healer.

> *"Daughter, you took a risk of faith, and now*
> *you're healed and whole. Live well, live blessed!"*
> Mark 5:34, MSG

Chapter 14

STRENGTH

I opened Instagram to see the post.

Someone my age was celebrating their engagement. I gulped, typed "Congrats," and went about my day. The next day, someone got promoted. A couple of months later, someone else took a job I had really been secretly wanting but decided not to apply. On most occasions, I scroll mindlessly and unbothered. But for some reason, in my weakest moments, Satan knows where to hit me. I started becoming increasingly discontent with what the people around me were doing for the Kingdom. I decided I was just going to unfollow or hide the posts of people who were doing better than me, and that way, I wouldn't be insecure in my own calling.

Unfortunately, when God starts working in my heart, He seldom lets it rest until the work is done. In a moment of quiet time with Him, He tenderly asked me if I trusted Him with the calling He had placed on my life to be free from the opinion of others. I claimed to walk in freedom, but that wasn't the case. I had one small part of my heart taken captive by the enemy's lies that I would never be good enough, and those lies had grown a lot larger than I was willing to admit. I forgot that we all were working for a common goal, which was the advancement of God's Kingdom. All of these achievements were like salt in my spiritual wounds, and as my heart dried out, my bitterness grew. I had started thinking and believing my kingdom was the only one I was advancing.

As a kid, I had always struggled with comparison. As an adult, social media fueled the comparison complex with a healthy dose of controlled stalking. I laid awake at night filled with open sores of hurt, bitterness, and wounding. Ultimately, the hurt turned to extreme criticism, as I started evaluating someone else's life through a computer screen. I bet they aren't really that happy, I thought, as I scrolled through their feed, all the while missing out on a family gathering in front of me. I scrolled my way through real-life because I had bought into the lie that scrolling was where I would find satisfaction. Ultimately, I realized, at the root of my ugly-hearted scrolling was fear. I was afraid someone would be more successful, receive more praise, and I believed the lie that someone else's unrelated success automatically negated all God was doing in my life. Instead of focusing upwards on what God is doing in our own lives, we start looking side to side at others' accomplishments, and that's how the enemy traps us.

There are days when my fear tries to crush me before I get out of bed. Whether it's crippling anxiety or doubt, I find myself aware of a whole lot of shortcomings. I get caught in wishing I had someone else's life, and I forget all about the promises God gave me for mine.

Once we start down the rabbit trail of someone else's belonging, we'll have to fight the lies of the enemy to feel content with ours.

The verse 1 Timothy 4:11-14 (MSG) very clearly gives us instructions for focusing on our calling.

> *Get the word out. Teach all these things. And don't let anyone put you down because you're young. Teach believers with your life: by word, by demeanor, by love, by faith, by integrity. Stay at your post reading Scripture, giving counsel, teaching. And that special gift of ministry you were given when the leaders of the church laid hands on you and prayed—keep that dusted off and in use.*

Whoa. It's like we're supposed to focus on our lives only and ignore the comparison traps the enemy sets before us. If we focus on what God is doing in our lives, we start to run faster towards our calling than ever before. When we're

STRENGTH

free of distractions and comparison, we will find ourselves a lot more caught up in what God is doing around us.

But can I be honest? That's harder than it looks. Growing up in church hearing, "Don't let anyone put you down because you're young," made me think I had something to prove. By being a young business owner, leader, and Christian, I felt the weight of my age directly tied to my reputation. I started becoming consumed with other people's opinions of my "young-ness," and I would do anything to make them think I was older than I actually was.

At work one day, someone started questioning one of my techniques, and instead of responding with the knowledge I had researched, I shut down. Instead of using my experiences to further advance the Kingdom and get the job done, I fell into the trap that my age automatically disqualified me. I've spent my whole life until a few years ago trying to disprove my young age by combating those comments with success or intelligence. In some ways, I felt like I missed out on enjoying my youth because I was so insecure about it. Ultimately, I realized my youth was a badge of honor. If God could call David from such a young age to be king, He could call me to do great things for the Kingdom, regardless of how old I was at the time. Instead of letting your age cripple you, wear it as a badge of honor as you run towards your calling.

On the other hand, I also fell into the trap that not letting anyone put me down automatically included the right to look down on others. Instead of joining together with co-workers for the advancement of the gospel, I decided I was going to be the best. The thing people don't tell you about being the best is you're the best all alone. Success via putting others down isn't the success God calls us to achieve. As Paul says, the only thing we are called to is to "stay at our post" (1 Timothy 4:13, MSG).

Your post might not make the most Instagram-worthy content, but it's the most peace-giving, fulfilling one you can have. The art of showing strength is showing vulnerable places in order to grow. When I was finally able to open up and say that I had success but was crippled by loneliness, I found freedom to be who God had called me to be. When success mattered less, my heart found peace by getting off the pedestal on which I had placed myself. My journal from that stage included this prayer:

> *"My soul has come to a crossroads. I can either show vulnerability, swing wide the gates, or drown in the waves of fear of failure. I've given it all. My job, my family, my future. I never want to give someone a reason to say, "I told you so," and it's killing me. Jesus, help me to give up my fear of failure. Give me joy because I'm finally ready to be utterly dependent upon You. Help me to embrace the honesty of who You've called me to be. I'm so tired of living in fear. Help me to trust You have good things for me in Your perfect timing."*

Here is the truth I know:
- Jesus' strength and power will do all the heavy lifting along the way.
- His glory is the prize we grab at the finish line, not our own.
- This race isn't about you.
- Community is essential, not seasonal.

Be brave enough to say you can't do it alone, and watch God's strength fill your shortcomings with joy.

Reflection Questions:

1. How are you doing things in your own strength instead of God's power?

2. What's something in your life that you're trying to do alone but you know you need to do with the help of others?

STRENGTH

3. How can you exchange your shortcomings for God's strength and joy today?

I'm not everyone's cup of tea, but I might be their Vashti

The story of Esther always intrigued me as a kid. How could God call this seemingly unknown girl to such a big task? I heard in church God can call you to do anything; you just need to be brave and be ready. When I grew up, God quickly became real. I realized the story of Esther was not just about the girl who God plucked from anonymity; there were more layers to it. Digging into the story, it's not just about a girl who becomes queen and saves her people. Instead, it's about a major role change; a queen steps down when her time is done and paves the way for a redemption story for an entire group of people.

I once worked in a church as an assistant to a pastor. I was young, severely impressionable, and had intrinsically wrapped my belonging into the amount of serving I did there. That led to a lot of sleepless nights, filled with anxious frenzying, as I compared my accomplishments of the day to the amount of love I thought God had for me. I worked there for about two years, and honestly, it took a lot of seeking the Lord, counseling, and amazing mentors to untangle the lies from the truths in that time period. I remember quitting the job under the guise of graduating college, and truth be told, I had cut back on my classes in order to keep up with the demands of the job. But I quit out of shame. I felt I

The Wild Calling

could never be good enough to earn God's love. I had turned serving God into a game of earning brownie points with Him daily.

My servant's heart withered away in that place. Exhausted and overworked, I sought comfort in the stories of God's equipping, calling, and encouraging His people. In the passages of Queen Vashti's story, I found permission to say "no."

I discovered that instead of the charge to keep pressing, I found a question from the Lord. "If your faith was conditionally based on your ministry, was your faith ever that strong?" This left me looking for strong women of the Bible to keep me going. I was drawn to Esther, initially, for some comfort to keep pressing on, but instead, I was drawn to Vashti. The reason I did not want to leave that job was because I didn't fully believe someone else could do it as well as I could, which was a lie from the enemy. There were tons of people well-equipped to do my task, but as I thought about it, jealousy swept through my heart.

I wanted to hoard God's glory for myself. Vashti wanted to hoard the king's glory for herself.

The two of us should get coffee sometime. Check out the story below to see why.

On the seventh day of the party, the king, high on the wine, ordered the seven eunuchs who were his personal servants (Mehuman, Biztha, Harbona, Bigtha, Abagtha, Zethar, and Carcas) to bring him Queen Vashti resplendent in her royal crown. He wanted to show off her beauty to the guests and officials. She was extremely good-looking. But Queen Vashti refused to come, refused the summons delivered by the eunuchs. The king lost his temper. Seething with anger over her insolence, the king called in his counselors, all experts in legal matters. It was the king's practice to consult his expert advisors...
Esther 1:10-15, MSG

Vashti's refusal to come to the king was a decision based on wisdom because she knew it was not where she needed to be. Instead of being regarded as a wise choice, to remove herself from that situation, it was viewed as rebellion. Our wisdom can be interpreted as rebellion when our orders are issued by someone who has lost focus. The position was given to someone "better" than her, but their version of "better" simply meant they were initially seen as more compliant.

As we keep reading through Esther, that isn't the case. Compliance doesn't equal ability. Eventually, the king's anger subsided, and he set out to find her replacement, and even though Vashti's wisdom cost her the title of queen, it didn't cost her God's plan for her life. We don't find out what happens to Vashti, but she used her wisdom to remove herself from a situation that could have cost her everything. Even though my wisdom to walk away from my serving until I could sort out the holy and the hurt was hard, God never wastes our pain. He always has a plan, even when we try to take His glory in the middle of it. Vashti's story had to happen for Esther to enter the scene, and while I don't ever want to think I'm the "Act 1 extra" to God's main character, sometimes it's the close of one of my chapters that opens a new book for someone else. Instead of becoming bitter that someone else got all of the glory, in my mind, I have to be reminded that God sometimes removes us from situations for His glory and not our own.

Friends, let's be cautious in this story. It was so easy for me to leave the church I worked at, feeling angry and bitter at God using someone else to do great things, but I believe that my great things were still being worked on. The key is to not let yesterday's wounds muffle the distinct sound of God's calling for today. It is easier said than done, but we must push past our desire to compare, to see the crown God has created specifically for us.

My encouragement to you is to pray for the people to whom you compare yourself because you're both fighting an enemy, and it isn't each other. For when we compare, we rob the Kingdom of unity and strength that is desperately needed to fight the lies of the enemy.

The Wild Calling

Reflection Questions:

1. Who do you compare yourself to?

2. What's something you can ask God to grow you in instead of comparing that grown gift to someone else?

3. What are some giftings you can be thankful for and not compare to others' gifts? It could be your willingness to serve, your kindness, or your ability to love people as Jesus does. List some of those things below!

Let It Rain

If I'm honest, I tend to shame the rainy days in my life. The days where I'm having a rough moment, need a break, or am otherwise frustrated are when I struggle with comparison the most. Everything looks bigger when the microscope is only focused on me, and the sad thing is I fall victim to it more than

STRENGTH

I admit. Bitterness doesn't just affect one area of life. It burns up the field of passion, leaving the heart charred and scared where flowers should've grown. Why does the ugliness in our hearts continue to grow? Why does bitterness towards old hurts take root in our hearts? God's glory is more than sufficient for more than one ministry. We can thrive without struggling to take from each other what we feel is ours.

The beautiful truth to our wait is this: God never makes us wait out of spite.

Your bitterness towards others and your discontentment with your skills and gifts will get in the way of your calling. You don't have to run in a pack to define your worth, but loving others well can't be done when you're isolated. Isolating yourself to keep yourself safe will only lead to more hurt than being vulnerable. Let the light in, and watch the shame fall away. Pick up any pieces of brokenness you've hidden along the way and bring them to the Father. He is working on behalf of your best interest. When I struggle to be bold, this psalm reminds me that asking the Lord for strength is where I will find the courage to run on His wild calling.

> *The moment I called out, you stepped in;*
> *you made my life large with strength.*
> Psalm 138:3, MSG

God, I'm really frustrated with your timing. I'm lost, weary, and so weak from fighting the Enemy's lies. I feel surrounded. Jesus, I need you to take over. I'm giving up.

This prayer was written in my journal several years ago. I can read it now and still feel the anguish.

I had just walked out of the most horrible experience with someone who I'd thought had my back. I was betrayed, broken, and ready to give in to the lies that I would never be good enough, pretty enough, smart enough, or qualified enough. In my heartbreak, I cried out to the Lord. I had nothing to give, and so, I was ready to quit.

But God showed up in that season.

God showed up like He has in every stage of life and changed the narrative. He held my broken and scarred heart, calling me beautiful, worthy, and so incredibly loved. Through heartbreak and wounding, I had lost every ounce of who I was to God, and instead, focused on who the world said I was. But God knew exactly what He was doing, and He picked me up from my hurt and taught me who I was in His eyes.

I'd like to say healing and strength are glamorous. But like a much-needed cry or a hard workout, it's not cute or "Instagrammable." Turning brokenness to strength is a quality that the Heavenly Father possesses, and the work He starts in us will be completed. Sometimes strength doesn't look pretty, but the ugly layers that the Lord reveals are very necessary to our growth. God doesn't call us to look the best on this wild gospel adventure, but He does call us to finish. Whether we drag ourselves over the finish line or we run across with arms pumping in victory, He is glorified. If your healing is taking too long in your eyes, look for where God is working. Even if all you see are shadows, don't lose heart. Shadows are just a sign that light is present.

When we can't see the promises for the shadows, we can claim the name of the One who makes a way through the dark. God isn't afraid of our weaknesses, and we shouldn't hesitate to surrender. Let's run this race with His strength, dear friend.

Reflection Questions:

1. Who comes to mind when you think of people who displayed strength in the Bible?

STRENGTH

2. When it comes to comparison, do you find yourself attaching your worth to what you do?

3. How do you think you can stop comparing yourself to others? For example, I limit my time on social media so I don't spend a lot of time endlessly scrolling.

4. Is there a specific thing for which you are asking God's healing?

5. If all you see are shadows today, I encourage you to write a Scripture out that encourages you in this healing time of life and place it somewhere you will see it.

CHAPTER **15**

The Thrill of Hope

One Sunday morning not too long ago, I was walking into church, and no one knew my name. After leaving a church where I also worked, I chose to visit places where very few people knew who I was or would interact with me. I was weary and tired of doing the things the Lord had called me to. I had a new job, a recent move, and even a new church. Frankly, I wasn't going to church to worship. Instead, I was eager to get out to my car as fast as possible after the service was over. I was going to church because I knew God wanted to heal my weary heart, but I would rather have kept it in the shadows. I was wary of starting the healing process and didn't really want to sort out the emotions I had buried with all of this change. Seasons of healing are not supposed to be idle times. When we feel dismal about the status of our broken hearts, we must remember where we came from and what God is molding us to do next.

"The thrill of hope, a weary world rejoices."[17]

Does the thought of a new stage of life make you weary? From the thought of a new move, a stressful transition, or a heartbreak, a season change can feel like a whirlwind. I hid from healing because I was afraid I would be the one running the show, trying to hold it all right there, and get my whole life sorted out on my own. I learned healing doesn't mean you're automatically thrown in front of a group and publicly shamed. When you hear the next step of your wild calling is a step of healing, trust God won't shame you. He might use this healing time

to reveal things about His and your natures, but He isn't trying to wound you further. So, when He calls you to trust Him in a new stage of life, know that He is actively working for your good and His glory.

Here's a truth I've learned during these times for a weary heart today:

Your invitation to walk into a new stage of life change does not automatically come with the burden of running the show. If and when God calls you to run the show, He will sustain the start, middle, and completion of that calling.

It's not about your ability to have the most decorated new home, the best church attendance, or the perfect Instagram photo. The purpose of studying, waiting, and healing isn't a hopeless chasing of worthiness, but a celebration of Christ. When we take the spotlight off ourselves, all of our tasks and to-do lists get a lot smaller, and we can finally let our weary hearts rest.

> *But when the kindness and love of God our Savior appeared,*
> *he saved us, not because of righteous things we had done, but*
> *because of his mercy. He saved us through the washing of rebirth and*
> *renewal by the Holy Spirit, whom he poured out on us generously*
> *through Jesus Christ our Savior, so that, having been justified by his*
> *grace, we might become heirs having the hope of eternal life.*
> Titus 3:4-7, NIV

In this weary season, find hope in the truth that it's not what you do; it's what He has already done. We can run to the throne and stay there. Our soul finds worth in Him and nothing else.

Reflection Questions:

1. Are there things in your life that make you feel more hopeless? Is it when you focus on what you have to accomplish in a day?

THE THRILL OF HOPE

2. A season change is the invitation to recognize all that Jesus has done for us, not the invitation for us to jump on stage and declare ourselves the director. What things have you found yourself trying to control during this time of life?

3. You can celebrate where God has you without running yourself ragged. Take a minute and list out all the things you've committed to for the next month.

4. What are some things you do that bring you joy? They could be anything from cooking, to being in your room listening to worship music. Find some time today to make a list, and then compare it to your to-do list. Are you doing things out of obligation or out of joy?

5. Is there something on your list you can cut loose? What can you decide is an "accomplishment" versus a "joy" in this period of life?

He is with Us

As modern Christians, we have a joy the Israelites did not hold in the early days of the Old Testament. One of my favorite songs makes me think of what they were poised waiting for, with just rumors of Jesus-not Jesus revealed. They had promises and prophecies of a Savior, but we have the fullness of God displayed in the fulfillment of Jesus before us. Jews were holding their breaths for the restoration of Israel, not realizing Jesus came to restore their souls. God's plan was so much bigger than their hopes. How much more would they have rejoiced had they known the Savior walked with them? The shepherds and wise men ran to Jesus, and they rejoiced in the promises fulfilled. We have the Holy Spirit living within us as believers, and yet we find ourselves racked with anxious thoughts. This is not the way we were called to live.

"O come, let us adore Him."[18] This Christmas song beckons us towards discovery of who God is, whether it's the Christmas season or not. We can learn a lot about adoration by putting ourselves in the Israelites' shoes. Striving creates stress, but adoration is joy in its purest form. Adoration is what we are called to in this life, with wonder and awe of how our Savior poured out for us.

Christ came into this world to save us, and He came to free us from what we burden ourselves with every day. Worry is something the enemy tries to cripple us with during a stage of transition, from stress about our families to financial woes. What if we saw this occasion, whatever it might be, as a spiritual holy ground? A place to declare His goodness and find joy in every moment. This season change could be the place where you get the healing you need for the wild calling God has in store for you. If this stage of life feels heavy and hard, cry out praises to the Lord, and watch His hands work in all your situations.

The Thrill of Hope

> *And they were calling to one another: "Holy, holy, holy is the Lord Almighty; the whole earth is full of his glory."*
> Isaiah 6:3, NIV

The angels called to one another, praising and adoring our Creator, as should we.

If you're struggling to praise or adore your Creator, ask someone else for help. Grab a wise sister or friend today, whether that be on social media or face-to-face, and take a moment to praise the Lord for what He is doing in your life. In the long run, the adoration of our Savior and all He has done for us, will create an atmosphere of joy in our hearts and homes in this time of change.

Focus on Jesus, and joy will come.

Reflection Questions:

1. How does spending some time doing things that bring you some joy change your perspective?

2. Is there one specific thing looming over you at this stage of life that steals your joy?

3. One of the most significant things I struggle with during times of change or growth is anxiety. I will wake up in the middle of the night panicked over simple things like whether or not I have the perfect gift for someone. Do you have a similar fear? If not, what is one of the biggest "mind-consumers" for you?

4. I've learned that the root of my anxiety is a desire to be well-liked. If I'm well-liked, that means that God must like me too, right? Wrong. My works do not mean God loves me more, and my desire to please comes from a hidden root of pride. Have you ever felt like you had to do good works for God to love you? If so, when?

5. How do the people around you make your new place of change fun for you?

6. The people that make your life changes fun are your tribe. List them below, and give a few of them a call or text and let them know how much you love them.

7. After talking to your tribe, take a couple minutes, and try to plan something fun for all of you to do. If schedules or distance are an issue, at least commit to call each other once this week, or form a group chat, and encourage one another.

THE THRILL OF HOPE

Though the Seasons Change

When I think of season changes, I try not to just think of the changes I don't enjoy; instead, I try to remind myself of the ones I do like to participate in. For me, a change of life can be an actual change of season-the arrival of the holidays. Starting around mid-October, Christmas music is playing, and I'm already putting my tree up in my home. The holidays always bring up warm, cozy images in my mind. Hallmark movies, commercials, and other advertisements always portray people wrapped in blankets, drinking hot cocoa, and so in love with each other. These are the living changes I look forward to most.

What I've learned is these transitions can often put expectations on others, and so we need to be careful how we view the people around us during times of good or hard growth. While those Hallmark moments can exist around the holidays, we often place unrealistic expectations on our family and loved ones to deliver those "Hallmark" moments in our lives. When we place our desire for love in others, it can oftentimes wound us when people don't live up to our expectations. Our loved ones are human, just like us, and they can fail or fall short of what we want them to do. Ultimately, we find love in new places in life when we take time to look at God, who will never fail us.

"For God so loved the world that he gave his one and only Son, that whoever believes in him shall not perish but have eternal life."
John 3:16, NIV

We recite John 3:16 from memory, like a chant, but do we ever stop and think what His unfailing love really means for us? The most valuable gift someone can give is themselves, and that type of sacrificial love is what Jesus accom-

plished. God would sacrifice His only Son for us, the ultimate display of love we can find. Are you surrounded by people who may or may not love you well? Hold tightly to the truth that you are immensely loved by your Heavenly Father. The truth is this: Hallmark movies pale in comparison to the love of God.

Reflection Questions:

1. How did your meeting last week with your tribe go? Journal some thoughts and insight into that gathering here, whether it was face-to-face or online.

2. Right now, resolve to remember that God's love is the only love that ultimately matters in your life. Whether you're single, dating, or married, you are loved. Leave your desire for love at His feet, and know that you are cherished by Him. How does your current period affect how you see love?

5. Who are some people that are easy to love in your life? List them here.

6. Who are some people that are hard to love in your life? It could be an estranged friend, family member, or co-worker. How do you think God is calling you to love them right now?

7. After making your two lists, look at them. Pray, and ask the Lord to highlight one person from each list to help you bless this week. It could

be anything from a text, lunch, or mailing them a card. It can sometimes be easier to feel God's no-holds-barred love in our life if we reciprocate that love into someone else's life.

God Doesn't Make Garbage

My desire to chase a dream can oftentimes be crippled by my fear of being vulnerable. If I let people know that I'm passionate about something and fail, does that really mean I was called to do it in the first place? When that happens, we start to circle our dreams, afraid to step inside the calling, in the hopes God will make them look a little bit more realistic or remove them completely. But here's the thing: He doesn't. Instead, He draws us in, closer to the thing we are most passionate about but also the thing we are most scared to chase. You know why? Because when we remove ourselves from the dreams we're called to chase, when we sit out on the sidelines in a self-assigned "waiting season," we stop waiting on God to move and instead wait on ourselves to grow the confidence to get back in the ring again. God didn't make us wait this long. We chose to prolong the wait in order to work through or justify our fear.

But the waiting, whether God-ordained, or self-inflicted, teaches us something. It teaches us to pursue Jesus in every stage of life. It teaches us to practice the rhythm of rest. Of gaining some traction in order to step back into holy ground. My wait isn't mainly about what I do in it but what Jesus molds me into. When we're ready to pursue Jesus in the wait or in the harvest, that's when we know we're ready to chase our dreams. My passion is only fueled by God's call, and if I'm not pursuing Him, my fire goes out. Therefore, we have to learn to pursue Him whether the fire roars or there are just embers. The God of the burning bush is also the God who watched over the Israelites while they wandered the desert for forty years.

There are so many times we've stopped a conversation, a text, or something big, like a book or a song because we're afraid there's one person in the world who thinks our ideas are absolute garbage.

Guess what?

There were people in the world who thought Jesus' teachings were garbage. Did that stop Him from doing His ministry, fulfilling what He had been sent to do? Praise God, it didn't stop Him or deter Him one bit! At one point or time, Jesus was rejected by everyone in His life. His followers, his friends, and even his Father. When that happened, what did that do to His ministry? Nothing. He still died on the cross, rose from the dead, and provided a way to the Father.

Here's the secret I've learned that is a life-turning truth: the rejection Jesus experienced, while painful, made Him better at ministry. He still loved people, healed the sick, and taught wherever He went. The rejection He faced didn't make Him run back to being a carpenter. I would have. One Pharisee would've sent me all the way back home and into my workshop. I'd have waited until it was safe again to continue my ministry. Maybe by the time the sting of rejection had died down, the Pharisees would have moved on to another target. However, my Jesus was not fazed by man's rejection.

If I spend my life being fazed by man's disapproval of me, or allowing my fear of rejection to dictate my calling, I'm spending time focusing on the lack of freedom I've created for myself by boxing my God-sized dreams. The cross didn't fit in a box. It was a calling Jesus walked faithfully, even when he felt rejection to his core. My dreams, if they are God-breathed, don't fit in my box. If I chip away at them, compromising my calling for safety, I can cram them in, and forget about them for a while, but the call on my life won't be contained for

THE THRILL OF HOPE

long. Instead of playing it safe and tiptoeing around our holy ground, why not run towards our dreams, pressing in and pulling others out of their benchwarmer positions on the sidelines?

Our call to holiness has more power than any man's rejection of us.

Let that truth permeate our safety nets, the ones we've set before God and others in order to avoid being hurt. This wild calling isn't safe, and there's so much freedom in living that truth. Holiness and hope can be simultaneously found when we walk forward into times of change. If you're feeling discouraged, I cheer you on in this stage of life. God is by your side working all change for good too. Whatever you are called to do in this moment, relax and let God handle it. We can't do it on our own, and we shouldn't want to. Hope and peace come when we let Jesus set the calling for our lives. All we have to do is show up ready to go.

In 2 Corinthians, Paul says, "But he said to me, 'My grace is sufficient for you, for my power is made perfect in weakness.' Therefore I will boast all the more gladly about my weaknesses, so that Christ's power may rest on me. That is why, for Christ's sake, I delight in weaknesses, in insults, in hardships, in persecutions, in difficulties. For when I am weak, then I am strong" (2 Corinthians 12:9-10, NIV).

Throughout our lives, we will have difficult times, when nothing seems to be going right. When we walk away from our dreams because we fear rejection, we shut down the part of us where hope can grow. God placed a compass in our hearts, one made to find truth north in Him. The world tries to distract us or deter us, whether by throwing good things or hard things our way. Whatever the circumstances may be, it seems to all hit when we are at our weakest, and it continues to batter us down. God does not say that our lives will be trouble-free, but He does guarantee that whatever happens, it is for His glory. If you're feeling battered down, use these scriptures to encourage you in this period of hope-finding.

We have to hold fast to the faith we profess (Hebrews 10:23), and look to the Lord for strength (Psalm 105:4).

Clinging to God is the only guarantee we have in this world. Standing on God's promises is an excellent way for us to combat whatever happens in our lives. Some great promises from God that can help in times of trouble are:

> *"The Lord your God is with you; the mighty One will save you.*
> *He will rejoice over you. You will rest in his love;*
> *he will sing and be joyful about you."*
> Zephaniah 3:17, NCV

> *"God is the one who saves me; I will trust him and not*
> *be afraid. The Lord, the Lord gives me strength and*
> *makes me sing. He has saved me."*
> Isaiah 12:2, NCV

> *God, your love is so precious! You protect people*
> *in the shadow of your wings.*
> Psalm 36:7, NCV

These are just a few of the promises God offers in His Word to those in times of trouble. As Sarah Young says in her book, *Jesus Calling*, "When the road before you looks rocky, you can trust Me [God] to get you through that rough patch."[19] Trust in God to get you through any time of despair or need, and believe in His promises for your life. One of my favorite verses reminding me God is in control and I need to trust Him is Philippians 1:6: "*For I am* confident of this very thing, that He who began a good work in you will perfect it until the day of Christ Jesus" (Philippians 1:6, NASB, Emphasis Added). This promised completion is good, just as He is good. Our completion might not be the prettiest or the most glamorous, but it will be for His glory. In this, we have the hope He will not let us go, and He will walk us through these times.

Peace is one of the things we all seek during times of change, and we try to find it in any way possible. When we see the hope we have in Jesus Christ, the joy we find in Him, and the love He shows to us all, we can live a peaceful life, knowing all we need is found in Him. We can run towards our wild calling, not because we are great, but because the One who called us is great within us. When you find yourself fighting discouragement in seasons of change, ask God

THE THRILL OF HOPE

for His perfect peace. One of my favorite songs is "Peace" by Hillsong Young and Free, and it serves as a reminder that His promises bring peace, even when everything is chaotic. I encourage you to listen to it today and be reminded that all our anxieties bow in the presence of Jesus.

All of His promises of hope, love, and joy translate into peaceful living when we claim them and walk in them. Scripture says we can be led in peace, and that helps us walk every day full of praise. Isaiah 55:12 says:

> *For you shall go out in joy*
> *and be led forth in peace;*
> *the mountains and the hills before you*
> *shall break forth into singing,*
> *and all the trees of the field shall clap their hands.*
> Isaiah 55:12, ESV

Peace can be found by looking to Jesus and keeping our eyes fixed on Him. In this time of change, when you're searching for purpose, remember that hope, joy, love, and peace are all found when our eyes stay fixed on our Savior.

Reflection Questions:

1. Journal here the results from your exercise on love. How did the Lord guide you to respond?

2. How do you find peaceful moments during a time of change?

3. Do you think social media plays a role in your anxiousness? Why, or why not?

4. Is there one area of your life that steals your peace more than the others?

5. What are some practical ways to create peace in that stressful environment?

6. This week, write some verses about peace on Post-It notes, and place them strategically in the areas where anxiety tends to flare up. If you get anxious on the go, change your phone background to a Scripture on peace! These simple reminders can help quell your anxiety by reminding you of the peace Jesus promises.

Chapter 16

New Year, New Me

I have a love-hate relationship with fitness. I joke that God created me to love people and food really well, and the second is easier than the first. I love the community that happens around a table, and I'm just now starting to untangle negative views around fitness and over-eating. I used to tie up my accomplishments with working out with how much food I could eat afterwards. The park I used to run at had a McDonald's on my way home, and instead of enjoying the run and then moderately enjoying McDonald's at another time, I ran so I felt worthy enough to eat fast food. I'd do this until I got discouraged, stopped running, and convinced myself I should just eat whatever I wanted and move on. This would happen until November each year. I would feel awful emotionally and physically, and I'd make it my resolution to eat healthier. I've since learned that when the first of the year would hit, I'd feel the urge to dig out my workout clothes, and start the vicious cycle of running towards earning something. As Christians, running because we want to earn something can look completely different in various parts of our lives. The first of the year starts, and we start running- running towards goals, resolutions, and trying to shape ourselves into the people we resolved to be. But why do we run? We aren't called to run all these little sprints so that we earn things, but rather, we're called to run a life-long race with heavenly goals.

We get so caught up in accomplishments and goals, and we place our identity in the things we do, rather than whose we are. I'm not writing this as someone

who has it all figured out. I've placed my identity in Christ but struggle to keep it there some days. For example, my identity can be found in work. If I'm successful and doing well, then I feel good about myself. My identity can become juxtaposed with my work, and then I start to place my identity in my work and not my Savior.

The first instance can be a way I give glory to God, thanking Him for the business He gives me and moving on to loving others out of the overflow I have received. When my "running" serves as a way to get what I deserve, however, it no longer pleases God. When we put our identity in something other than Jesus, we shortchange our walk with Him and shortchange our ability to walk out our wild calling. If our identity is found in something other than what God has called us to, we're going to be a lot more hesitant and less willing to run with purpose. In my own life, my calling is to run on a mission and to empower people to live out the fullness of their calling that God has given them.

For me, calling looks vastly different when my identity is found in Christ as opposed to when it is found in other things. In order to correct this desire to run towards other things, I want to dive into what it means to place our identity in something other than Christ, and learn how to rest who we are, solely with our Heavenly Father. God has made us run toward our wild calling, and I wouldn't want to run towards anything else. Paul reminds us of this in Ephesians, when he says, "For we are God's masterpiece. He has created us anew in Christ Jesus, so we can do the good things he planned for us long ago" (Ephesians 2:10, NLT). If we are new creations, minted in God's image, we are called to run towards the things that will bring glory to Him and nothing else. So, instead of running to earn something, run as a masterpiece toward your wild calling, and don't look back.

Reflection Questions:

1. What do you think of when you hear the word "identity"?

NEW YEAR, NEW ME

2. Have people in your life told you or shown you what they place their identity in? It could be money, work, school, or even family.

3. When you know your identity, it is a game-changer in your walk with the Lord. How confident are you that your identity rests in Him?

4. Is there a place in your life in which you wish you had more confidence?

5. Take some time today to jot down things people say about you or things you do. Pray, and ask the Lord to show you if you're placing your identity in those things.

The Wild Calling

The Banner of Truth

In college, I worked full time in a church, worked an almost full time job as a barista, and worked as a real estate assistant. I would spend the fifteen minutes in between jobs coordinating a dog-sitting or babysitting job on my "free night" of the week. It was so exhausting, but I felt it was necessary to succeed. When I moved out of my parents' house to become a "real" adult, I packed up a lot of emotional baggage as well, and the heaviest thing I took with me was the banner that said, "YOU CAN NOT FAIL." I had grown up with the notion that failure was the worst thing that could ever happen to someone, and if it happened to me, I would be worthless. Instead of looking at living on my own as a new experience and giving myself space to struggle, I flew the banner of my inability to fail in every room. Through God's gracious humbling and running out of time to function, I learned I was going to fail. I was going to accidentally throw away my debit card, not know how to turn the water heater off vacation mode when I moved into my first house, and sleep through my alarm a few times. All of these things and so many more happened, and the banner that screamed I couldn't fail, or I was worthless, got a lot louder.

Eventually, the humbling that took place was painful because I had fought it for so long, but God's graciousness helped me come to a key realization in my wild calling adventure: my identity cannot ever be found in anything other than Jesus. When my identity is found in anything else, I shift my life to justify my decisions.

I shifted my life to justify my belonging and worthiness. I based it on what I did and how much money I made instead of walking in confidence. God was not honored in that stage, nor is He honored in any time period where we let

NEW YEAR, NEW ME

insecurity run the show. If I place my identity in anything other than Jesus, and He calls me to something and I say *no*, I walk away from my wild calling. I miss out on an opportunity to walk in closeness with the Lord and develop my relationship with Him further because I'm telling God what I will and will not do for Him.

Can I be honest, friends? I have struggled with the fact I don't have a degree in writing or ministry. I have a degree in digital marketing, which comes in handy, but doesn't look as "holy" in other people's eyes when you tell them you are running towards a calling in ministry. As much as I love it all, from theology to Hebrew and Greek word studies, I don't have training in any of those. This doesn't mean I'm incapable of leading or pursuing this part of my calling. Instead of trusting and stating the Lord has called me to something, I try to over-educate myself in order to be more "qualified."

Education is not wrong, and in some cases, God uses it as a launching pad for our wild calling. When we agree to things like education or a career, it does not mean we are using them for our own selfish means; instead, it means we must seek out discernment as to what our motives are. It just means I have to make sure my identity rests in Jesus, instead of in the pursuit of being "qualified." I used to feel that if someone ever said to me, "Can you even do this?" I would have to rush to defend my calling. I used to justify the calling I felt God had placed on my life in many ways. I was the last one to leave the office, to finish studying, or to leave the church. Honestly, I was tired! God peeled open the layers of my running to reveal the insecurity I held with my calling, and He's poured truth into the wounds and lies I've believed- that I'm not good enough or qualified enough.

Now, when people ask me what I feel called to do, I don't have to ask them to agree I'm qualified. I just have to trust. I can state I'm qualified because of who my Heavenly Father is, and that's enough for me.

The truth is, if my identity is found in something other than God, I will take time that is not God's timing to prepare myself and qualify myself. If God has called you to write, and you feel like you should be educated before you pursue it, by all means go for it! But if God has called you to launch something in

The Wild Calling

your heart and walk it out in an act of physical obedience by starting a ministry, starting a blog, leading worship at your church, or speaking, don't be afraid. In other words, don't pull a Moses. Moses was called by God to lead His people out of Egypt, but when God told him what was needed, Moses found seemingly great excuses as to why he wasn't the guy for the calling. Exodus 4, illustrates how Moses sought to get around God's calling for his life because he didn't feel qualified. It serves as a lesson for all of us.

> *But Moses said to the LORD, "Oh, my Lord, I am not eloquent, either in the past or since you have spoken to your servant, but I am slow of speech and of tongue." Then the LORD said to him, "Who has made man's mouth? Who makes him mute, or deaf, or seeing, or blind? Is it not I, the LORD? Now therefore go, and I will be with your mouth and teach you what you shall speak." But he said, "Oh, my Lord, please send someone else." Then the anger of the LORD was kindled against Moses and he said, "Is there not Aaron, your brother, the Levite? I know that he can speak well. Behold, he is coming out to meet you, and when he sees you, he will be glad in his heart. You shall speak to him and put the words in his mouth, and I will be with your mouth and with his mouth and will teach you both what to do. He shall speak for you to the people, and he shall be your mouth, and you shall be as God to him. And take in your hand this staff, with which you shall do the signs."*
> Exodus 4:10-17, ESV

Whoa. It's easy to see what I mean by "don't pull a Moses." Don't sit in the presence of God and say you're not equipped and try to send God someone who is more "qualified," according to you. The world is full of people who are more equipped than me, but they don't have my calling. The truth behind this story is God doesn't call the most qualified people, but He calls the people who will bring glory to His name. If I place my identity in anything other than Jesus, and He calls me to something and I say no, I miss out on an opportunity to walk in closeness with the Lord and develop my relationship with Him further because I'm telling God what I will and will not do for Him. Once we acknowledge our calling, we must respond with believing and action. That is what makes it wild, the notion that we follow Jesus securely instead of having it all figured out. When we act on this wild calling out of security instead of seeking people's approval, we find the freedom we've been searching for all along.

Reflection Questions

1. How did your exercise from the last questions go? Write your observations here.

2. In what ways do you justify a misplaced identity in your life? For instance, have you wrapped your worth up into something you're doing?

3. How are you pursuing your calling first and foremost over making knowing your Savior your main priority?

4. What is one area in which you would like to improve when it comes to your relationship with the Lord?

5. Have other people ever mentioned to you that you're "obsessed" or "consumed" with something?

The Wild Calling

Identity Crisis

When it comes to identity, we can take our identity way out of context and control. All through high school, my identity was based on good grades and remaining a straight-A student, and I decided that moniker of perfection was who I was supposed to be. I tried teaching because someone told me I would be good at it. I worked in the service industry because I was told I was good at it, and I found out I had surrounded myself with the opinion of others instead of the opinion of God.

I thought I was called in that stage of life to bring others joy by pleasing them with how well I could do in school, work, or everyday life. One of my dearest friends was actually intimidated by me in high school because I sat by myself and read books all day. She interpreted this extreme act of social isolation as a form of pride by way of removing myself from social settings and growing in my education. What she didn't see was a small, insecure girl who was desperate for someone to look past her GPA and see her desire to belong.

In all of my striving, every A+ I earned made the pressure mount. I was making great grades, but I was also extremely anxious and very overwhelmed. My entire senior year of high school and freshman year of college was plagued by the worst anxiety of my life.

I pushed myself to breaking-point trying to be a person I was never called to be. I was never called to carry the torch of other people's dreams and, simultaneously, box-up mine and put them in the corner, telling God I'd come back to them later. Working through my constant desire to please people and control my life on my own has really allowed me to see how much my heart was desperately made for Christ.

I joke that I used to be smart (I still enjoy learning and education), but I got a C in a class my last semester of college, and I rejoiced because, in the grand scheme of things, *God's Kingdom is not won when I break myself or sacrifice my peace to win the approval of another person.*

If you're still learning what God has for you and your life, don't hold yourself to another person's grading scale. God's call is so much better than your perfect ACT score. Learning to remove the idols of school and perfection really have helped me hear what God is telling me to do. Once we can realize we don't live for other people, it can help us find out what we're supposed to do. We will learn to hear the heartbeat of the Father over the noise of the crowd.

> *Am I now trying to win the approval of human beings,*
> *or of God? Or am I trying to please people? If I were*
> *still trying to please people, I would not be a servant of Christ.*
> Galatians 1:10, NIV

What a beautiful reminder. We are not here for us. We are here on Earth to glorify God, and in order to do so, we have to remove the idea God is pleased when we shrink ourselves down to submit to what other people want for us. One of the wildest things I have learned from God is His covenant with us is one that frees us from others' expectations and helps us focus solely on His will. In 2 Chronicles 13, a covenant of friendship and provision is brought up in a seemingly random place during a battle between two kings. Abijah and Jeroboam were fighting over who controlled the kingdoms, and Abijah went on top of a mountain to proclaim, "Listen, Jeroboam and all Israel! Don't you realize that God, the one and only God of Israel, established David and his sons as the permanent rulers of Israel, ratified by a 'covenant of salt'—God's kingdom ruled by God's king" (2 Chronicles 13:5, MSG)?

God's kingdom established a line of kings, and apparently, Abijah thought Jeroboam needed the reminder. Israel and Judah had split, and Jeroboam had rebelled against Solomon, which in this context, was like rebelling directly against the Lord. This covenant of salt appears only four times in the Bible, with only one mention in the New Testament. I bring it up because God used it to show me something beautiful in my frantic seeking. A covenant of salt symbolizes a few things. In the Old Testament, salt was used as a preservative and as a flavoring for the people wealthy enough to afford it. Therefore, it was only brought out during special times, such as offerings to the Lord or at meals with close friends and loved ones.

Through the continuation of the line of David via Jesus, we have access to this promise of salt. We are promised through the provision of salt God will never fail us or let us go unpreserved. Salt also reminds us we have access to a close friendship with God. I know salt today is considered a flavoring for food, but in the Old Testament, it was used as a symbol of friendship and provision. It symbolized friendship because salt was something so hard to find that one only used it to season special meals shared with friends. It was considered a sign of provision because it was hard to come by, so if you had it, it meant God had blessed you abundantly.

God made two covenants of salt, one with the line of Aaron, Moses' brother, and one with the line of David. God had promised a covenant of salt with the line of David, so any act of rebellion meant the friendship and provision afforded to this line was removed. This was all easy for me to overlook in my walk of faith, but as I combed through the Old Testament one night, in desperate need of promises to claim, this one promise of provision stuck with me. If you're struggling to see God's plan over other people's expectations in this moment of your wild calling, know He has wrapped you in a covenant of protection and friendship with Him. We cannot outrun our Heavenly Father, and His providing hand will lead the way. Choose what He calls you to do, and trust the details to Him.

NEW YEAR, NEW ME

Reflection Questions:

1. Is there an area in your life in which you feel others' expectations have too much influence on your decisions?

2. In what ways are you seeing God provide for you today?

3. Is there a specific person or group of people in your life that you feel have more influence than they should?

4. When we put our focus on other things, it causes tension between our calling and our desire to do what we want. Have you ever experienced this?

5. As followers of Jesus, we have been given the gift of the Holy Spirit to help us with our struggles. Spend some time in prayer, asking God to help you pinpoint places where you have given in to the opinion of others, and ask Him for wisdom to follow His truths.

The Wild Calling

Lost in the Woods

When I was old enough to drive, I loved taking the nearest backroads and getting lost. It was a way for me to spend time with God and lose cell service, therefore losing all distractions. As a senior in high school and unsure of what God had for me, I took these roads quite frequently. I was searching for a safety net, a familiar road, or path in a time where I felt like I was always on the alert for somewhere to hide. One of these adventures led me to find and hike up a local small mountain, where I learned the meaning of finding refuge in God. I parked my car, angry with God, and started marching up this mountain.

God had not revealed His plan for my future quite on my timetable, and with financial aid deadlines and college applications creeping up, I was honestly mad at His snail-like pace. Just like the trail on this mountain was cut out, I felt my next steps should have been as well. I got to the top and asked God, "Why can't my life plan be this clear?" I selfishly snapped a couple pictures for Instagram because whether I was mad at God or not, it was still a beautiful view. I then started making my way back down the mountain. In my furious, one way conversation with the Lord, I had failed to notice how dark it had gotten. Yup; I was on a mountain at dusk, and my only interest was getting off before I became stuck up there for the night.

In my hurry to get back down the mountain, I jumped off the trail to speed things along, which of course, only worsened the situation. Long story short, I ended up seven tenths of a mile from my car, and in the backyard of a less-than-friendly mountain man. In east Tennessee, that's still a thing.

I was scared, sore, and still angry at God, but I learned a valuable lesson that

NEW YEAR, NEW ME

day. *Whatever* you do, do not get off the trail. Ever. I look back and laugh now, but I have never gone back to that mountain since that incident. When I found the path to walk, I could see clearly what I was supposed to do, but when I took matters into my own hands and got off the trail, that's when things got bad. In life, the same thing happens. When we keep our identity in Christ, we can more easily see what God has for us as we walk faithfully with Him. When we take life into our own hands and go running off the trail, that's when we get hurt. When our identity is found in Christ, everything changes.

One of the basic needs of people is shelter. Nowadays, we have fairly easy access to suitable housing, but in ancient times, one of the most reliable forms of shelter was caves. Before we all freak out and think about dark, gross, wet caves, these caves were not so. Many caves were places of safety, solitude, and refuge, and the people who ran to them were secure. Isaiah talks about the people who run to caves, saying, "they are the ones who will dwell on the heights, whose refuge will be the mountain fortress. Their bread will be supplied, and water will not fail them" (Isaiah 33:16, NIV).

When people needed shelter and rest, they found a cave. When we need to rest our identity somewhere, we can place it in the shelter of our Savior. Just like sheltering in a cave, placing our identity in Christ is a sure thing. Caves don't move, and neither does Christ. He is a solid foundation and someone we can run to for comfort in our times of need. Our Abba is our Rock, and in Him, we find rest from the world and security in knowing where our identity is found.

Here is my encouragement to you: when the world gets loud and wild, run to your Refuge. Keep your identity safely stored in His cave, and watch how you feel safer, lighter, and more equipped to conquer the everyday battles you face. When we no longer carry the weight of determining our own identity, we are much more useful and effective warriors for Christ. Knowing we have a place to run makes us more motivated to fight the battles before us.

Caves are not a place of isolation but of safety. Placing your identity in Christ is not going to isolate you. It will instead empower and free you. In the next couple of days, focus on where the Lord has placed you at this time in your life and start to pinpoint the parts of your identity. We are only free when found in Him.

The Wild Calling

Be gracious to me, O God, be gracious to me, For my soul takes refuge in You; And in the shadow of Your wings I will take refuge Until destruction passes by.
Psalm 57:1, NASB

Reflection Questions:

1. How do you feel your relationship with God allows you to find refuge in Him?

2. What hinders you from coming to God when you need Him?

3. In what ways do you think God wants you to find refuge in Him over finding it in other things?

4. What are some other things in which you find refuge? A relationship, a friendship, money, or good grades?

5. If you can, set aside time with the Lord to spend reading Psalms, and study where the word refuge is found in the Bible. Read how He provided every need and was a place of refuge for David. Know that He is a place of refuge for you. My favorite verse about refuge is found in Micah:

NEW YEAR, NEW ME

But as for me, I watch in hope for the Lord, I will wait for the God of my salvation, My God will hear me.
Micah 7:7, ESV

Less is More

When your identity rests in Him, you can breathe deeply. Anxiety will cease, and fear disappears as you learn to live your life from a place of refuge rather than a place of striving. I am so thankful for the grace the Lord has shown me as I constantly learn how to leave my identity fully found in Him. I pray this study helps you launch your calling. Say *yes* to what God has for you. Just breathe deeply. Rest like David, who knew who he was. You are fully known and loved by God, and that is the most secure place to be.

When it comes to our identity, **less is more**.

When we narrow down the things we place our identity in, it allows us to walk our callings with clarity and peace. If you're struggling to know God's calling for your life, start by learning to hear His voice. This year, spend intentional time learning how He speaks to you because **He is speaking**.

You are chosen. You are loved. You are found.

The Wild Calling

*But you are a chosen people, a royal priesthood, a holy nation,
God's special possession, that you may declare the praises
of him who called you out of darkness into his wonderful light.*
1 Peter 2:9, NIV

Reflection Questions:

1. As chosen people of God, we are called to walk in God's call for our lives. Do you feel like you're currently walking in God's calling on your life? Why or why not?

2. This last assignment is lengthy, so carve some time out if you can. Write down a prayer to God, asking to hear from Him every day this week (or as often as you can), and then spend fifteen minutes listening. No music, no phone; just absolute silence. Normally, when we quiet our environment from the clamor of the outside world, the Lord speaks in mighty ways.

CHAPTER **17**

BEAR WITNESS

As spring approaches, gorgeous weather is around the corner, and we are starting to shake ourselves from our winter slumbers. Homes get spring cleaning, friends adventure out into the world, and we begin to chase new journeys in our lives. I'm not a gardner by any means, but I do love seeing the growth that comes after the previous winter. I struggle with feeling winter is never going to end, and the dreary days wear on me, until I see that first flower start to bloom. Spring can be an extremely healing and fruitful time, but it is important to discuss what God is calling us to proclaim in a time of new growth. As Christians, making sure our hearts awaken from a potential slumber to speak life to people around us is essential to our relationship with Jesus and His calling on our lives.

Jesus is incredibly specific in the book of John about the concept of bearing witness and being sent out. Throughout His entire ministry, He was constantly calling and equipping His disciples, which includes us, to bear witness to His name. When we live our lives with Kingdom vision, we begin to see Jesus in every step of the way.

There was a man sent from God whose name was John. He came
as a witness, to bear witness about the light, that all might believe
through him. He was not the light, but came to bear witness to the light.
John 1:6-8, ESV

John the Baptist was the voice to awaken the Jewish people from a spiritual winter spent waiting for the Messiah-over 400 years of slumber. He was intentionally formed by God, created to call attention to Jesus as the Savior of the world. Another incredible part of this story is Mary, the mother of Jesus, and Elizabeth, the mother of John the Baptist, were cousins. I firmly believe God uses families to bear witness to all He is doing, and He is doing it in your family if you're willing to speak His words. We are called to bear witness, just as John the Baptist did, and to shine the light of Christ onto the people around us. For me, that starts in my family.

Growing up, in the form of the women of my family, I had the most beautiful examples of people who would bear witness to what God was doing in their lives. This specifically came down to my mom, Mam (short for Mammaw), and my Aunt Paula. I watched these women walk through cancer diagnoses and treatments, raising a special needs child, and dealing with traumatic brain injuries. I have journals of prayers of God's faithfulness and promises from my mom, messages and books from my aunt, encouraging me to find joy in the middle of sorrow, and many nights spent with Mam, eating way too much chocolate and talking through the hard questions in life. When I think back on the people who have been bearing witness to what God was doing in their lives while also pointing out where He was moving in my own, I think of these three women. If you are reading this and think of someone who does this for you, I encourage you to let them know. My gals are pillars of God's faithfulness, and I cannot repay the blessings they have heaped on me over the years.

On the other hand, *family* is a hard term for some people to hear, and I do not believe we are called to stay around bad people or situations if they are hurting us. However, God can use us to bear a witness of redemption to even the most difficult family members. Redemption and bearing witness starts in families, so, one of the most important things to pray through as you seek your wild calling is, "How can I live my life bearing witness to Jesus to the people around me?" Just as John the Baptist rejoiced about Jesus and spoke God's Word to prepare a way for the Messiah, we are called to live our lives speaking God's hope and truth to the people around us.

When I first thought through the concept of being called to bear witness, I came at it from an extremely isolated mindset. I thought bearing witness was supposed to be done alone, but I am so thankful God has taught me what it really looks like. Community is important in the mundane and the holy moments alike. We are supposed to find people to do life with who feel like drinking from a well; people who remind us to go to the Well of Living Water. Let Him fill you in every moment as you bear witness to His name.

How do we live bearing witness to Jesus? The Greek word for witness is "martus" and is actually where we get the word *martyr* in the English language. John, as the Scriptures states, was clearly sent by God to prepare the way for Jesus. He bore witness and ultimately gave his all. John gave his life for the calling to bear witness to Jesus, and while many of us are not called to give our lives, we are called to give what we have with a sacrificial heart.

Having a sacrificial heart is often blown out of proportion by social media, and watching other people highlight how they live for Jesus on the internet, can often leave us discouraged and defeated. While we're called to bear witness to Jesus and sacrifice things for Him, the Kingdom is not won when we display our calling for our own personal gain. Inflating our ego does not get us any closer to Heaven. If you are struggling with discerning what is your own ego and what is the call of God, ask the people around you who are bearing witness to what He is doing. With careful prayer and discernment, God will lead you to a clear understanding of what it means to bear witness to Him and how to surround yourself with others doing the same. Ultimately, we are called to bear witness to others, and we are to love them unselfishly and sacrificially, as Christ loves us.

Reflection Questions

1. How do you live bearing witness to Jesus?

The Wild Calling

2. Does your everyday life reflect that you follow Christ?

3. Is there one area of your life where you struggle to bear witness to Jesus? A job, a friend, or a relationship? Write it here, and for one week, consciously pray over that area.

4. In order to bear witness to Jesus, sometimes we have to give things up. The Holy Spirit could prod you or ask you to give something up this week. Just be mindful and prayerful to hear what that is.

5. Is there an area in your time with the Lord that you struggle to hear from Him or find yourself distracted? It could be during prayer, Bible reading, or journaling. Once I get started journaling, I start writing down my grocery list or random to-do's that come to my head. While this might be productive, it is distracting me from hearing the Lord. If you struggle with this in your quiet time, be intentional to stay focused on what you're trying to do. Play some instrumental worship music, or light a candle, but most importantly, eliminate distractions so you can hear from God.

Chapter 18

WHERE ARE YOU STAYING?

Jesus turned and saw them following and said to them, "What are you seeking?" And they said to him, "Rabbi" (which means Teacher), "where are you staying?" He said to them, "Come and you will see." So they came and saw where he was staying, and they stayed with him that day, for it was about the tenth hour. One of the two who heard John speak and followed Jesus was Andrew, Simon Peter's brother. He first found his own brother Simon and said to him, "We have found the Messiah" (which means Christ). He brought him to Jesus.
John 1:38-42, ESV

At first glance, the disciples' interaction with Jesus in John 1 may seem like a quick conversation. Jesus turned to the disciples following Him and asked them what they were looking for by following Him. At second glance, we can notice a couple important things in this above text. First, the callings of the disciples happened fairly quickly after Jesus' baptism. Jesus didn't waste any time delaying the calling. This still rings true for us today because once we are commissioned, we cannot survive as young Christians, if we delay our calling. The call to follow Jesus was one of motion, and while that was a wild concept to some, Jesus was not fazed by the spiritual mileage He was calling others to log. Jesus was curious to see the level of commitment in the disciples, and their reply not only answered this, but it encouraged Him. The first question

was basically, "What do you want from me?" and the disciples answered, "To find home with you." These men were lost, weary, and needing a purpose. They found it and so much more.

The question we have to ask ourselves as believers is, "What are we seeking from Jesus?" Are we following Christ for personal gain, or are we following Him because He is the one who called us? As a realtor, my number one question for people is, "What are you seeking in a home?" Many people answer with their dream house list: the perfect yard, a spacious kitchen, or a master bathroom with a jacuzzi tub. These are all wonderful things to find in a house, but when I ask what they are seeking in a home, they struggle to put it into words. Are you seeking a place to raise a family who plays baseball in the backyard? Are you seeking to make your home the place where your high school freshman girls' small group gathers every Sunday, and you pour truth into their hearts? Are you seeking the presence of Jesus to fill every room of your home as you seek healing from your past?

A house is just a structure, but the difference between a house and a home is in the intent of the use. A house can serve as a structure of shelter, but making a home takes practice and cultivation to bring your wild calling into the rooms you occupy. What type of journey are you seeking when you follow Jesus on this wild calling? I've discovered what I'd like to seek is actually quite different than what God calls me to on a daily basis, so at the end of the day, I've come to this conclusion: all I want to seek is Him and let the rest follow. When it comes to this world, what are you seeking? Are you looking for fame, followers, or peace? Most people crave the spotlight, but as stars and celebrities have confessed, it isn't all it has been cracked up to be. Instead of searching after the spotlight, I am making it the highest priority on my wild calling ride to bear witness to Jesus alone. The rest will fall into place, and I'm perfectly content with that.

I absolutely love word studies. In John 1:41, Andrew says, "We have found Him." In Greek, the word for "We have found Him" is *heurekamen*, which means to discover something after searching. What Andrew was speaking of was they had found the Messiah, the one to fulfil all the promises of the Old Testament. This phrase is one full of hope, and I am left in awe of how these

WHERE ARE YOU STAYING?

promises have come to fruition. The one man who was called to bear witness, prepared a way for this very moment, the realization of the promises fulfilled in Immanuel. When we search like the disciples, we find what we are looking for, which is Jesus. He is waiting to be found, if we just look up from ourselves for one moment and look to Him.

Reflection Questions:

1. What brings you peace in your life? Take a couple moments to write it down.

2. How have you gotten away from the things that bring you peace? By overwhelming your schedule or crowding your mind with unnecessary thoughts? Take a moment to sit before the Lord, and discern what has stopped you from following your calling.

3. If you feel a bit trapped in a certain situation in your life and feel like that is holding you back from living life as Jesus calls you to, write that situation here.

4. If you're dealing with a situation or circumstance that is making it hard to change how you're living for Jesus, commit to praying about this for a week. Name the promises of God over it, and watch as your perspective changes.

5. How has your quiet time changed since you started focusing on searching for Jesus? Are you finding yourself less distracted?

Come and see!

"Come on in; the water feels great!" I froze at the end of the diving board. As a kid, at the beginning of one summer, I went over to a friend's house to try out the pool for the first time that year. I always forgot how warm the water actually was, and how deep the bottom of the pool looked from the diving board. I froze, not sure if I should jump in or if I should retreat back to where all the grown-ups were sitting. Unfortunately, my younger brother saw it as the perfect opportunity to push me in the not-so-cold water. Once I was in the water, I then became the biggest cheerleader to get everyone else in the pool. I think this rings true in our walk with Jesus. Sometimes, we hesitate to jump in to the next thing He has for us on this wild calling, but once we do, we spend the rest of our days trying to get others to follow suit. After finding Jesus, we must invite others to join us.

The feast at Cana has been touted as Jesus' first miracle in ministry, and it can be a great model for our starting point in running life on mission for Jesus. When we seek God in the celebrations and the mundane, we find He is there performing miracles in the middle of it all.

WHERE ARE YOU STAYING?

Now there were six stone water jars there for the Jewish rites of purification, each holding twenty or thirty gallons. Jesus said to the servants, "Fill the jars with water." And they filled them up to the brim. And he said to them, "Now draw some out and take it to the master of the feast." So they took it. When the master of the feast tasted the water now become wine, and did not know where it came from (though the servants who had drawn the water knew), the master of the feast called the bridegroom and said to him, "Everyone serves the good wine first, and when people have drunk freely, then the poor wine. But you have kept the good wine until now." This, the first of his signs, Jesus did at Cana in Galilee, and manifested his glory. And his disciples believed in him.
John 2:6-11, ESV

Jesus' miracles created belief, brought on by proof, and were sustained by His nature. What that means is, His miracles piqued curiosity about who He was, when the people around Him saw the fruits of His miracles. Just like Jesus drew people in to believing in Him by showing them the fruit, we are called to do the same. Drawing others to the nature of Jesus starts with bearing witness to all He has done in our lives.

Something I noticed in this story was that Jesus never said how full to fill the jars. Out of our doubting, we can "fill" our jars with maybe a cup, or even half-way full, but Jesus rewards the things that are done to the fullest. We have to believe that even when we give our all, Jesus is there waiting on us to empty ourselves in order to be filled up. Just as the servants filled the jars to the brim, Jesus waits to fill our lives to the brim if we allow Him to do so. Opening up every part of our lives for His fullness can be painful, but God sent Jesus to remove our sin in order to give us fullness. Let's take a dive into the pool and believe He will not let us be harmed. Jump off the diving board, let go of what's holding you back, and swim into all He has for you.

Reflection Questions:

1. What is something in your life that you're asking Jesus to fill up? It could be free time, energy, joy... Take a couple of minutes and write it down, Tell why!

2. What is stopping you from bringing your jars before the Lord?

3. How do you think God feels about your empty jars?

4. How would you live your life with "full" jars? Would you be more joyful, laugh more, or just have peace?

5. Jesus was sent to save us and to bring us fullness of life. He didn't come to condemn us but to call us to greater things. This week, consciously bring your empty feelings, like jars, before Jesus, and watch Him fill you up.

CHAPTER **19**

IT ALL MAKES SENSE

In college, I had this cute, sporty, Toyota Yaris. I say it was sporty because I drove it like Cruella Deville, and unfortunately, I had the speeding tickets to prove it. While my driving was something worthy of shame, I was stuck in a mindset that said my time was more important than anyone else's on the road. This led to some unfortunate run-ins with law enforcement. After a hefty $300 ticket, I either had to change my mindset or hire an Uber. When I asked the Lord why I drove like I had total ownership of the road, I think He must have smiled. He kindly reminded me I was taking out my frustration with Him on the other vehicles. I felt stuck in my life, stuck in traffic, and stuck in a place of waiting on God. I was impatient and just needed to feel seen, even if it meant being seen by law enforcement as I sped through that stage of life. I'm so thankful the time of speeding tickets and impatience is behind me, but I'm also thankful for the things the Lord taught me in that place.

Have you ever been mentally stuck? I was more than just stuck in a lead-foot mindset. I was stuck in extreme impatience with the Lord. My ministry was moving at a slow pace, and I was frustrated with what God wanted me to do about it. I was doing all the "right" things when it came to leading and ministering to others, but where I saw soil ready to explode with fruit, God saw ground in which I was to pause and learn from Him. This period of being stuck was not introduced to be frustrating, but those were the emotions I processed. I wrote in my journal at that time: *God, I don't want to surrender and trust. I want to push*

and make this all work together exactly how You called me, and to see the fruit today. Help me to change that desire to push. If You called me to this season to ask me to surrender, I give it all.

Ultimately, I realized I was not being held up out of cruelty from the Lord; instead, I was being kept safe in my waiting. My desire to be seen drove my emotions and actions until the Lord brought me to this realization though. I wasn't being called to go backwards, for there was glory in the occasion right in front of me. At the end of the day, I realized my desire to be seen by others, remove myself from situations I was stuck in, and to move onto greater things, meant I was trying to bypass the growth God had for me. I didn't realize growth came when I gave up my agenda for how my wild calling should look. If you're in a similar place with the Lord, can you commit to one thing? Instead of the busy, surrender; instead of the worry, surrender; instead of trying to make it work on your own, surrender. What would this next stage (eg. the next three months) look like if it was fully surrendered to God? Sometimes when it comes to sitting in the presence of God, our purpose is not always to discover something new. Oftentimes, it's when we are reminded of the words of truth He's already planted in us, and we need to be surrendered to hear them.

When I worked in a church, I watched a lot of really amazing people do the "hosting" for our Wednesday night services. It was normally one or two extremely high-energy people who would go on the stage and do a giveaway, a game, or just get everyone excited for the service. I watched some extremely talented and called people do that job night after night, and a small seed of envy was planted in my heart. I wanted to be like these people, fun and vibrant. I believed a lie that if I was the person who was seen the most by others, I would be the most loved by God. So, when the opportunity came up for me to co-host one of these services, I jumped at the chance.

In complete honesty, I've done a lot in ministry, but I wasn't good at everything. Hosting was one of those things, and if I'm honest, I still cringe at the thought of it. I now know why God made a difference between extroverts and introverts, and that night helped me realize. I got on the stage and fumbled over my words; constantly messing up the announcements and then just awkwardly standing there on stage waiting for it to be over. This experience is forever in-

IT ALL MAKES SENSE

grained in my mind when I start to envy someone else's gift, and this has since given me a huge respect for people who do this work as their calling. I also walked away with an understanding of the term "bloom where you're planted."

A common misconception in the church culture is we are called to "bloom where planted" because if we are planted in a specific role, it must mean we're called to it. When we sign up to serve in a new ministry, and it doesn't feel right, we are often told to keep on because serving God is what we "should" do, regardless of where it is in the church. And yes, we can honor God while we're there, but when He calls us elsewhere, or when we voice feeling unsatisfied where we are, a lot of people tend to make comments such as, "Well, you just need to bloom where you're planted." This well-intentioned phrase is one passed down from choir members, to children's workers, to small group leaders, and while they mean well, ultimately, we are called to serve where the Lord leads, not where all your friends serve. Those two might be the same thing, and when that happens, it is a beautiful thing, but oftentimes, we can start to sense that the Lord is replanting us to where we can grow in our giftings.

If you sense a tugging in your spirit when you serve in a specific area, explore where the Lord leads you. Ask for a week or two off from your normal serving responsibilities in the church to try serving in another area. Blooming where you're planted only works if God planted you there, not if someone is keeping you there out of need or selfish motives. You will not bloom, or continue to bloom, unless God places and sustains you somewhere.

One of the first ways to discern where God wants you to go in a time of waiting is to ask yourself, "Are my goals close to the Father's heart?" If your goals are to be noticed by others, or to hide a hurt in your heart with busyness, then I encourage you to spend time with the Lord cleaning out the clutter in your heart. The cluttered parts of our hearts are like the junk drawers in our homes. If I throw every little thought in the junk drawer in my heart, over time, it becomes overcrowded with things that don't need to be taking up space there in the first place. Whatever you want to accomplish, bring it to the Father first. Give Him your fears, dreams, and goals, and trust His hands at work. Ask Him to clean out the junk drawer in your heart and help you figure out the wild calling laying underneath all the clutter. Practically, this looks like journaling out what you're

The Wild Calling

currently involved in at church or in your life as a whole. Evaluate how these activities make you feel as you participate in them, and make note of some things:

- Does this activity make me feel fully like myself? Do I have to become a different version of myself or a different person entirely to participate?

- Does this friendship or relationship feel forced or unnatural? Do I walk away from time with this person encouraged to pursue my wild calling or encouraged to pursue something else?

- If I spent the rest of my life being fully alive in my wild calling, would I do this? If not, why am I doing this?

How you answer these questions will help you discern how you're living life running towards your wild calling. Spiritual decluttering starts with creating space to be honest with God before you bring other noise and voices into the mix. That way, when you speak how you feel, God can answer back with the truths He's placed in your heart.

When I think of people in the Bible who lived their lives running towards God's wild calling, Ruth jumps to the front of my mind. I used to read the story of Ruth as a fairytale, but now I read it and see God's goodness for all it is fully worth. I'm obsessed with Ruth, quite frankly. She's one of my favorite gals of the Bible because not only does she remind me that I have to place my feelings up against God's truth; she reminds me that His promises are always around the corner. When I've striven for approval or lived life through how someone else wanted me to live, I was reminded of God's perfect plan of redemption for Ruth and found hope for my stage of searching for God to make sense of my wild calling.

Now Boaz had gone up to the gate and sat down there. And behold, the redeemer, of whom Boaz had spoken, came by. So Boaz said, "Turn aside, friend; sit down here." And he turned aside and sat down. And he took ten men of the elders of the city and said, "Sit down here." So they sat down. Then he said to the redeemer, "Naomi, who has come back from the country

IT ALL MAKES SENSE

of Moab, is selling the parcel of land that belonged to our relative Elimelech. So I thought I would tell you of it and say, 'Buy it in the presence of those sitting here and in the presence of the elders of my people.' If you will redeem it, redeem it. But if you will not, tell me, that I may know, for there is no one besides you to redeem it, and I come after you." And he said, "I will redeem it." Then Boaz said, "The day you buy the field from the hand of Naomi, you also acquire Ruth the Moabite, the widow of the dead, in order to perpetuate the name of the dead in his inheritance." Then the redeemer said, "I cannot redeem it for myself, lest I impair my own inheritance. Take my right of redemption yourself, for I cannot redeem it." Now this was the custom in former times in Israel concerning redeeming and exchanging: to confirm a transaction, the one drew off his sandal and gave it to the other, and this was the manner of attesting in Israel. So when the redeemer said to Boaz, "Buy it for yourself," he drew off his sandal.
Ruth 4:1-8, ESV

See, Ruth was passed up by her first redeemer but not her final redeemer. Also, shoes counted as legally binding objects in the Bible, and, in my opinion, should totally still count today. These are both great reasons to lean into this story. Few people ever talk about the first kinsman redeemer, but it was more than likely someone who was close to her, like a cousin. This cousin was expected to complete what God had set out for the Israelites to do, which would fulfill a covenant of honor, but he passed up marrying her and becoming her redeemer. Whether it was the fact he'd already had a plan for his life or just simply didn't want to marry her, she had to experience rejection in her life first.

Enter Boaz and enter God's great redemption story. In our lives, our so-thought redeemers might not be our final redeemer. The person who we think should love us might pass us up, the job that should be ours will go to someone else, or we might fail the class we need to pass in order to get the degree we've dreamed of since birth. These situations are so discouraging but not the end of the story. The truth is this, dear friend: our final redeemer (Jesus) is the one who will save us and sustain us in the end. This means we shouldn't strive for the first redeemer, but rather, we can rest in God and know our redemption is in Him. If the first good job, good plan, or good friend passes us up, God's not surprised. It will all make sense when we reject the clutter and lies and seek His wild calling first.

The Wild Calling

Reflection Questions:

1. Do you beat yourself up for your failures or when you believe Satan's lies?

2. What comes to mind when you think of God's redemption?

3. Are you involved in a community of believers that pushes you closer to Jesus? If not, I strongly urge you to find people you can do life with. It's the only way we survive as believers, by surrounding ourselves with people who remind us of God's goodness and grace.

4. Ask the Lord to search your heart and reveal where you are living out of striving instead of freedom. We are called to live free because of Jesus.

5. Write down what you think surrender would look like in this place of your life, and spend some time in prayer asking God what He wants it to look like for you. If you don't walk away with a clear direction, it's okay!

IT ALL MAKES SENSE

Waiting on God

For the Spirit to draw us closer to being more like Christ, some refining needs to take place. It's not a monumental event most of the time, rather small realizations that bring us one step nearer our wild calling. I recently went through one of these refining seasons and had to wait on the Lord, and I pray that some of the realizations from my experience help you when you wait on God to grow something beautiful in you. I've learned our feelings of loneliness can either push us closer to God or further into isolation, away from our purpose. One of the most beautiful Scriptures on waiting is Hannah's prayer in 1 Samuel:

> *Hannah prayed and said,*
> *"My heart exults in the Lord;*
> *my horn is exalted in the Lord.*
> *My mouth derides my enemies,*
> *because I rejoice in your salvation.*
> *"There is none holy like the Lord:*
> *for there is none besides you;*
> *there is no rock like our God.*
> *Talk no more so very proudly,*
> *let not arrogance come from your mouth;*
> *for the Lord is a God of knowledge,*
> *and by him actions are weighed.*
> *The bows of the mighty are broken,*
> *but the feeble bind on strength.*
> *Those who were full have hired themselves out for bread,*
> *but those who were hungry have ceased to hunger.*
> *The barren has borne seven,*

> *but she who has many children is forlorn.*
> *The Lord kills and brings to life;*
> *he brings down to Sheol and raises up.*
> *The Lord makes poor and makes rich;*
> *he brings low and he exalts.*
> *He raises up the poor from the dust;*
> *he lifts the needy from the ash heap*
> *to make them sit with princes*
> *and inherit a seat of honor.*
> *For the pillars of the earth are the Lord's,*
> *and on them he has set the world.*
> *"He will guard the feet of his faithful ones,*
> *but the wicked shall be cut off in darkness,*
> *for not by might shall a man prevail.*
> *The adversaries of the Lord shall be broken to pieces;*
> *against them he will thunder in heaven.*
> *The Lord will judge the ends of the earth;*
> *he will give strength to his king*
> *and exalt the horn of his anointed."*
> 1 Samuel 2:1-10, ESV

I know this prayer is long, but God put it on my heart in my time of waiting. While I didn't have a prayer for the bows of the mighty, I did have a heart desperate for God to hear my prayers. As I walked in the footsteps of someone who had their prayer answered by God, it didn't instantly change my outcome, but it did change my confidence. I pray that prayer like a battle cry, claiming every good thing God offered Hannah as my own. I found when we approach the Bible with a heart that dictates terms for encountering God, we belittle the authority of His Word to move in our lives.

While this prayer didn't give me the exact desire of my heart during the waiting, it did give me a change in perspective while I waited. God used this time of waiting to show me specifically what my wild calling should look like, and He also used this time to grow the confidence to commit to what He wanted me to do next. So, if you find yourself in a place where you feel like God has intentionally held something back from you to grow something in you, find a prayer in the Bible and commit it to memory. Pray it when you feel discouraged, anxious, or when you need a reminder that God is working. Claim these prayers as spiritual markers in the ground, places where God showed up in mighty ways, and remind yourself He is doing the same for you. Take some time to ask the Lord a specific prayer to claim in this stage of life, and write it here.

Reflection Questions:

1. What prayer are you specifically claiming in this time of your life?

2. How can you invite others to pray this specific promise or prayer over you?

3. When you wait, what are some of the emotions you go through with the Lord? Do you look forward to the growth in the wait, or do you find yourself frustrated with the things you feel you're missing out on?

CHAPTER **20**

WHY WE NEED TO BLOOM

I can't grow plants. If I'm honest, I can kill a cactus in a week, and it's always been a point of embarrassment. I don't want to be the girl who admits she can't grow something, whether it's in life or in the garden. When I was sixteen, I started helping people build websites and run their social media accounts. When I was nineteen, I printed business cards. I hired an intern at twenty-one and had a full on "company." I worked so hard at growing my company to be great, but I pushed the calling to help people and serve in ministry down in the dirt because I felt more inclined to make money. I ran this business until about a year after I graduated college.

One day, God placed the strongest urge on my heart to sell my company. I was honestly stunned, not at the thought of selling my business, but at the thought of having to tell people I didn't keep going with the company and help it grow. I thought God's calling to sell the accounts was one of defeat instead of growth, and I justified my frustration by taking on more clients than ever before.

Over time, God, in His mercy, got me to a place of total humility and surrender by realizing that this was just too much for me to handle. I begrudgingly sold my business and chalked it up to a failure, burying the desire to help, with the desire to succeed. I struggled with the idea I couldn't make anything grow because I had watched things fail for so long. Eventually, I let the dirt from all the dead things get kicked over my wild calling and bury it all.

What I didn't realize is that when God called me to sell my marketing business, He wasn't doing it to crush me. Instead, He was doing it to free my purpose from my desire to be the biggest and best. Selling it freed me up to spend more time serving in the church, to dedicate myself to my full time job, and to spend time with people who filled me up and then encouraged me to pour out where I felt called, not just where I saw an opportunity to make money. When we feel buried, our purpose is the driving force that propels us out of our buried times and into our calling. We can't stay stuck in the soil forever, and God doesn't mean for us to stay there. We are supposed to grow in this wild calling adventure, and it all makes sense when we look at it from God's perspective.

How we grow is something I'm still figuring out. Growth is a hard thing because it's not just something you write down as a formula and hand to the next person, but rather, it is cultivated in a personal relationship with Jesus. Instead of giving you a formula for growth, I'm going to encourage you in this wild-calling life, to ask Jesus how He wants you to grow. Use tools such as the Bible, community, and encouraging resources, but ultimately, the God who made you knows how you're meant to grow. Fruit trees don't just bloom and stop. They continue to grow, gaining nutrients and pointing upwards towards the sun, getting strength from its light. Eventually, they produce amazing fruit from their flowers.

Our places of growth are often redemption seasons. By the time we enter a redemption period, we've brought our anxiety to the light, and spoken out our God-sized dreams, the ones that scare us, but also get us out of bed in the morning. Just as God was faithful to Hannah, He will be redemptive in my life. He doesn't half-do or half-promise anything to us, so trust that when you pour out your heart to Him, He is working. Knowing the will of God and His wild calling for our lives comes from the transformations that take place in our hearts. As people who crave knowledge, we desire to justify how God is working, but instead, He calls us to have childlike faith while He works in our lives far greater than we can imagine. Surrendering to His good plan is the first step in our wild calling starting to make sense.

In 2 Kings, Elisha went back to the Shunammite woman's home and told her to leave because of a famine in the land. She left, and after seven years, returned and asked the king for her land. Since it had been so long, the land had more than likely been taken over by someone else, but after hearing how Elisha had restored her son, the king restored her land. He stated, "Restore all that was hers, together with all the produce of the fields from the day that she left the land until now" (2 Kings 8:6b, ESV).

What blows my mind is she left out of trust, and God rewarded her trust with abundance and protection. She had no idea she would get her land back with abundance added to it, but she believed her God was good and He would take care of her. I love this story because when I get frustrated with God's timing, I remember I might not see His fruit for years, but I know it's there and waiting on me. Not only did she believe in restoration, she believed she would not be held back when she returned.

When brokenness or discord sweeps in, we have to claim what God has given us. He promises restoration and provision, even when we do not see where He is calling us to go. Friends, I know that blind trust is the hardest form of trust, but if we live our lives with our own strength we can sell ourselves on a safe calling rather than the wild calling we are intended to live. Our own strength will never build us back up when we fall down. I've come to realize being prepared in the waiting is one of the main purposes of the waiting, and while it is frustrating, we have to prepare for the goodness of God to be revealed.

When the Lord whispers something in the silence of the waiting, it becomes ingrained in our hearts and will not be easily forgotten when the world rushes back in. In times of waiting, the Lord has taught me preparation is key, and preparation takes time. As frustrating as that is, I find peace when I think God, the preparer of salvation, is the one leading my wild calling.

Reflection Questions:

1. Do you feel like you're living your wild calling today?

2. If you don't feel like you're living your wild calling, do you see patterns of playing it safe?

3. What do you sense that God is whispering to you in the silence of this moment in your life?

Let's get ready

It was 2011, and I was obsessed with Taylor Swift. I had all her albums and even had instrumental tracks where I could sing the words and pretend to be her. It was a time in my life when I loved music and wanted to become famous one day. I wanted to be on stage with Taylor and have all those fans cheering for me. In preparation for that to come true, I took voice lessons and even tried out for some TV shows where I could showcase my talent. The feedback I kept receiving was that I became too timid on the stage, even though it didn't look like that in my head. My voice was prepared, but my heart wasn't ready at all. I was scared of failing and had spent so much time preparing my voice, I didn't even bother to prepare my mind to be on stage.

Fast forward a couple of years, and I'm now leading worship at church, and no

WHY WE NEED TO BLOOM

longer struggle with the fear that gripped my heart. I had years to prepare my heart before the Lord, and all that has made my passion for singing stronger. In life, we can't just rush to the next thing we're called to do without making sure every aspect of our lives is ready. The places where we are supposed to sacrifice for the Lord (our altars) are supposed to be prepared, and it takes a waiting season to get them ready. Just like God had specific instructions for the Israelites to sacrifice to Him, He has specific instructions for how we are called to prepare our hearts and our lives. In living for Christ, we become examples for all people of his love.

> *"For even the Son of Man did not come to be served, but to serve, and to give his life as a ransom for many."*
> Mark 10:45, NIV

When we wait on the Lord, He begins to prepare a spiritual altar in our hearts, one where we can lay down our burdens and surrender fully to Him. For some people, it's the release of anxiety, for others pride; some confess hidden sins, but all come away from their altars and their periods of waiting a bit lighter than they entered their time with the Lord. Your place of preparation for your wild calling can be where God launches you into your next adventure for His Kingdom. Don't begrudge the preparation, dear friend. He is making something beautiful from your sacrifice and surrender.

When it comes to spiritual altars or times of surrender, it's completely alright if yours is not an ongoing publicly displayed altar. Sometimes, God calls us to surrender something privately and declare it publicly at a later time for His glory, and while redemption is exciting to shout from the rooftops, some people only want to trample your sacrifices to the Lord. Choose wisely, and pray for discernment when you feel led to share what God is calling you to surrender. Setting boundaries does not make you unholy. Allowing the voice of man to dictate over the voice of God is what makes it sinful. Surrendering to the Lord is most effective when you hear His voice first and only. Out of the overflow of your surrender, your wild calling is born.

When it comes to building a temple, the Old Testament laid out a lengthy process and steps for completion. I studied this process in seminary, and the pro-

cess showed me how He's shaping me on this wild calling. I've learned sacred spaces in the Old Testament took years to build, and God uses time to create places of sacrifice and encourage me as I walk through this current season and onto the next one.

The Israelites did not build large, elaborate temples in times of war or wandering. They made sacrifices on the go. There was no long-term temple until they settled in Jerusalem. When there was peace, they built beautiful elaborate temples, but until then, they grew in their faith. We can use stages of growth and change as opportunities to build our temples. Instead of focusing on the frustrating aspects of a stage of life, we have to realize when we build up our temples, it means sacrifices are coming. We are temples hosting the Holy Spirit, and our altars are being built in order to prepare our sacrifice. Building a temple in us means allowing the Holy Spirit to clean out the parts of our hearts that aren't reflecting His glory. When God builds a temple in us, it's to prepare us to run on this wild calling, whether we're running into a battle or into a time of peace. Either way, building a temple in our lives means intently leaning into the Holy Spirit to hear Him.

Temples built in war will not last because, in times of turmoil, they get destroyed. It is incredibly hard to take full advantage of hearing the voice of God when we are caught up in the battles raging around us. In a season of waiting, we can spend plenty of time hearing the Holy Spirit's voice to guide us. The wait is not supposed to be miserable, so when God gives times of waiting, take joy in it! It all makes sense when we realize that in the waiting and in the building of the temple, we have great hope. The Hebrew word for "wait" is *qavah*, and one of my favorite definitions is "to look eagerly for." When we are in the middle of the wait, we aren't just supposed to trod along, but rather, we look eagerly for God's promises to be revealed in our lives. Brick by brick, He is building something beautiful.

In places of waiting, it's easy to be idle and slip into the idea God is going to just "show up" one day and tell us what to do next. Instead of taking a backseat approach while waiting, I've learned to use this time to really learn the heart of God, which helps me to see His hand in my life more clearly. I use my Bible as an active tool to learn His heart. While waiting, we cannot treat our Bibles exclusively as museums to observe or manuals to study, but rather a combination of both. When we look at what God has done for others, we learn how to see His hands working. When we treat the Bible as a manual, we can learn practical life applications for our current season of waiting or for a season of sacrifice, healing, mission, or an abundance of all those things. We run the risk of missing the entire point of preparation during the waiting when we treat the Bible as something that has little or no value in our journey.

Standing firm in our roots is another aspect of our wild calling, and I think it's so important to realize our roots will make an impact on how we live our lives. When we stand firm, our roots grow deep, and that foundation will nourish us to complete our blooming.

I think sometimes we get so focused on what others are doing we can miss what He's doing right in front of us. In our wild calling, we find security in knowing we are exactly where we are supposed to be. When our souls make their home in Jesus, we find rest. This also frees us from comparing our own calling to others. Our lane to run is our own, and when we consume ourselves with what others are doing for the Kingdom, we eventually stop running our race. We aren't created to bloom as crooked or unhealthy flowers; we bloom from a place of nourishment and security found in being nourished by our calling, and no one else's.

Something happens when we try to do it all: we can't do it all well. When someone else gets put on stage, put on camera, or does something wonderful for the Kingdom, we shouldn't be offended by their success. Getting our feelings hurt easily or letting our pride rule our lives will not serve us on our wild calling. If we take offenses seriously when serving the Kingdom of God, we have to take the calling placed upon us with the same seriousness. If our pace is not the same as someone else's, we can find ourselves getting frustrated with the Lord's timing, but we don't have to move fast in order to move forward. Occasions when we are called to wait are not supposed to be idle. When we feel dismal about our wait, we must remember where we started. We aren't made to live out of striving to be like someone else, so part of it all making sense in our wild calling means figuring out what God specifically wants us to pursue.

In the moments when the noise fades, does joy remain? When you stop all you're doing for a moment, are you enjoying where God has you? Have you let pain, brokenness, or the desire to be loved shape how you pursue your wild calling? If anxious thoughts or bitterness are consuming you, I urge you to allow the Lord to clean that out of your heart. Healing is not supposed to be shamed, and sometimes, our greatest strengths are exactly what the Father grows from the broken places. Remain tender, even in your pain; this is where you find strength. The things you never think you'll be able to get over are exactly what the Father wants you to release and use for His wild calling. Through it all, even in pain, we can trust that He is faithful, and He is trustworthy.

> *But the Lord is faithful, and he will strengthen you and protect you from the evil one. We have confidence in the Lord that you are doing and will continue to do the things we command. May the Lord direct your hearts into God's love and Christ's perseverance.*
> 2 Thessalonians 3:3-5, NIV

Because of God's nature, we have confidence He works it all together, even pain. His love and Christ's perseverance sustain us when we're searching for understanding. If you feel heaviness lifted in this moment, know that God is working to bring together the next aspect of your calling- to bring understanding. If not, trust the Lord has your best interest at heart and is growing you more than you know! Just like Hannah wasn't alone in the temple, Ruth was not alone in the field, and David was not alone in the cave, we are never alone. We have the King of Heaven by our side yesterday, today, and forever. Our feelings of loneliness might be our perspectives, but they are not our situations, for we are never alone.

I've always loved songs which include verses from Psalms. Some of my favorites have been the songs of blessings and songs of reminders. I make it a point to memorize songs that have Bible verses in them, and if there is not one, I've been known to make one or two up. It's a great way for me to memorize the Word of God and also put worship deep within my soul at the same time. One of my favorites is Psalm 103, considered a "hymn song."[20] David was experiencing God's kindness in the later years of his life, and so, this hymn was a reminder to himself and was intended to be passed down to other generations.

WHY WE NEED TO BLOOM

Bless the LORD, O my soul,
and forget not all his benefits,
who forgives all your iniquity,
who heals all your diseases,
who redeems your life from the pit,
who crowns you with steadfast love and mercy,
who satisfies you with good
so that your youth is renewed like the eagle's.
Psalm 103:2-5, ESV

"Forget not all his benefits," has stuck out to me lately. Just like God was real to David, I've watched God be real to me in so many ways. God has been real to me for a long time in the capacity of childlike wonder and awe. Lately though, I've realized God becoming real to me is not a moment of Him being visible or tangible; it's a lifetime of acknowledgement of those factors. God is real in the days when life is 100 miles an hour, and a spirit of peace washes over me, and in the stillness of the night, when my fears are running wild. God has been real to me in the middle of panic attacks, family illnesses, and unfathomable heartache. God has also been real to me in moments of abundant joy, flowing into the day-to-day life that builds into moments of breakthrough. God is real to me in moments when I question His promises, and He is abundantly real when I find those promises again.

As a kid, I often reflected on how God made the world. I loved creating, from LEGO cities to building creatures out of Play-Doh, and I found my best examples of God in those moments. I cared so much about my creations and loved showing them off with pride to my parents and whoever else was available. As an adult, I've learned to shift the focus of my creation to my writing and my work. Just as God writes our redemption stories from start to finish, I'm learning what that process feels like on a daily basis. God is real to me when I look into the eyes of a loved one and feel immense pride and trust in them. God is real when I'm confronted with heavy and hard things, and His peace guides me through it all. He is real in the pit, in the good, in my sin, in His steadfast love and mercy. God's "realness" is evidenced in the air in my lungs and the calling that burns in my soul to spread the Good News to others. God is real in my confidence that can come only from Him.

God is real to me in my remembrance of all He's done, in my life, and in others. Whether you feel He is worthy of praise today or not, I encourage you to remember His goodness in your life. If you're struggling, feeling like He is not working, look back to all the times He has worked on your behalf, and let those moments make Him feel real once again. Forget not all His benefits, dear friend, and let Him show you His reality once again.

Reflection Questions:

1. When you look at a time of your life when you felt extremely frustrated, what do you remember about the roots of those frustrations?

2. When you're feeling stuck, what is the process you go through to get un stuck?

3. Have you ever been in a place where you served somewhere out of obligation versus serving out of your calling?

4. When you hear the phrase "bloom where you're planted," what does that mean for you?

WHY WE NEED TO BLOOM

5. As time allows, take a moment to ask yourself, "Are my goals close to the Father's heart?" Journal your responses here.

Chapter **21**

A NEW LEAF

You know the feeling a couple days full of rain brings to your soul? I was born and raised in east Tennessee, and the rain here is absolutely beautiful. The birds come out and chirp, you can watch the rain hit the mountains and head towards the valley, and it just fills your soul with satisfaction. This feeling quickly dissipates when you realize it's going to rain for the next six days. That feeling of longing for the peace the rain creates quickly turns into mud puddles and longing for blue skies again. Sometimes, our souls can become like a muddy lawn, full of good intentions, promises, hopes, and dreams that are just soaked by a little too much discouragement. This has been my story for the past few weeks and even past few stages of life.

I'll start something with good intentions-beautiful and in every way, shape, and form, exactly what God intends, and I'll watch it get mired down. I start to question, "Am I even hearing the voice of God? Or have I just misinterpreted Scripture to fit my own prideful agenda?" This is a valid question to ask for discernment, however, it is not the truth. Discouragement will creep in if we allow it, but most importantly, it will settle into the cracks of our souls-the cracks we've hidden from our Savior, and refuse to let Him fill. This leaves them open-ended and ready to flood..

This is not what the Lord intended. Rain brings promises of health, growth, happiness, and most importantly, a future downpour of the Lord's provision.

The Wild Calling

When these expectations are not found in our every day, and our lives are not full of the overflowing joy God so greatly promises, we can easily sink into despair and reject the future the Lord has for us. My friends, I'm urging you; don't settle for this. This minor flooding that has upheaved your sown grass is not the final stopping point. The sun will come out, the Lord will redeem, and you will bloom into the fullness of what He has for you.

> *Have mercy on me, O God,*
> *according to your unfailing love;*
> *according to your great compassion*
> *blot out my transgressions.*
> *Wash away all my iniquity*
> *and cleanse me from my sin.*
> Psalm 51:1-2, NIV

David had messed up. He had chosen to sin against God by taking Bathsheba to be his own, and when the weight of his choice fell on him, he was ashamed. I do not believe it was God's plan for David and Bathsheba to be together, but by God's grace and redemption, it worked out for good. David had hit a place of rebellion with the Lord, and it had less to do with him wanting to have Bathsheba as his own and more to do with him wanting something God didn't provide him (in his mind).

David's sin stopped being about a woman and became about rebellion towards his wild calling. He had been set apart from a young age, anointed by God, and he'd reached the point where that was no longer enough. Being set apart did not satisfy David any more; he had become addicted to the power that accompanied God's promise for his life. Once David believed the wild calling, he started to learn both the weight and value God had placed upon his life. Value came in the anointing that God placed on him as a king and leader of God's people. It had weight in the way it opened him up to responsibility, sin, and temptation, and as the story of Bathsheba illustrates, his responsibility did not always get handled well. In our lives, we will find temptation, but we can also rest on God's promises.

For us, carrying the wild calling has both weight and value in the Father's eyes.

A NEW LEAF

The value is the confidence to walk in your calling. What you carry also has weight, and that is the wisdom to walk in God's truth. There is redemption to be found when we're willing to surrender to what God wants over what we selfishly crave.

This Psalm is a journey towards redemption. David eventually stops justifying his sin and comes into the presence of the Lord with full humility, eager to be restored to a clean heart. God's love has many facets, and in this context, it is His *hesed* love, one full of loyalty and a reminder of His covenant of mercy. Just like David needed a reminder of God's covenantal love, this Lent season could be a beautiful time of reminding your soul that the One who created you loves you regardless of what you've done in your past. Take some time today to pray the verses David prayed, asking God for a reminder of His mercy.

My prayer for fighting discouragement is this: *Abba, as we walk through this season, help us to be reminded of your covenantal mercy, one that will never leave us even when we sin against you. Help us to remember your grace is the banner over our lives and for us to believe the beautiful calling you have in front of us.*

"This great song, pulsating with the agony of a sin-stricken soul, helps us to understand the stupendous wonder of the everlasting mercy of our God."[21]

In life, we quit lots of things. We quit habits, jobs, and relationships. Unless they are vices, quitting is normally regarded with negative connotations. When we quit a job, it's automatically assumed that there was something wrong with one aspect of the position. This can lead us to stay in places that are no longer meant for us in order to keep that negative connotation from being attached to our lives. Instead, what if quitting was regarded as a holy procedure? When we surrender, we quit our expectations. We quit our human lives when we commit to follow Jesus on this wild calling, or at least we quit what we think our lives should look like. When I pray about quitting something, I ask that God would always grant me the wisdom to quit in a manner of surrender, not of giving up. This is the part of quitting God wants us to get really good at doing. Just as the disciples quit their idea of fishing to become fishers of people, we have to quit the idea that our callings will look exactly how we've wanted to shape them.

The things we quit are not signs of failure. Rather, they are steps on a staircase with one goal in mind: to build us up as the person we are called to be, a person fully alive in the wild calling.

> *And I am sure of this, that he who began a good work in you will bring it to completion at the day of Jesus Christ.*
> Philippians 1:6, ESV

When we quit the things God calls us to quit, we start a relationship between the brokenness we carry and the Healer who wants to mend our brokenness. Quitting has nothing to do with failure and everything to do with surrender. God is going to complete what He's called us to start; it's our wild calling to get really good at quitting all the rest.

The easiest thing I've ever quit in my life was my first job. When I was fifteen, I decided getting a job would be the best way for me to grow up. I had always been a mature kid, and having a job was just one step closer to freedom. So, I waited until I was three weeks from being sixteen and called a local deli restaurant, minutes from my house, and applied with all the gusto one might give a corporate job interview. I think I even wore a button down shirt and dress slacks to the interview. I had no idea all this job required was the ability to wait at some small tables and run a cash register.

This job was so much fun in the beginning because of how "grown up" it made me feel, but I quickly realized it drained my tank faster than I could fill it back up. I'm an introvert with a tiny capacity for extroversion, so eight hour shifts of small talk made me slowly dislike this job more and more. After about six months, I started looking for some other job options, and thankfully, I found one. I turned in my two-week notice with just as much eagerness as I had applied for the job, but this time, I didn't even have the energy for the button up shirt and slacks.

That job taught me so much about finishing a task well, and I've always looked back on it with a respect for people who work in the service industry. I'm completely certain God called me to start that job, but I'm also completely secure in the fact I was supposed to quit. Discerning the voice of God over the fear I

A NEW LEAF

had towards quitting was a test of faith, but God is always faithful. He does not ask us to start things to fail them, but He does work all things for good, and that includes quitting.

Reflection Questions:

1. What has been the easiest thing for you to quit?

2. What has been the hardest thing for you to quit?

3. What is something you could let go of today that would get you one step closer to your wild calling?

4. If you're feeling a stirring in your heart from the Holy Spirit to quit some thing, I encourage you to seek His voice above all your fears. What are you afraid to quit doing or even cut back on?

5. If you can, write out what your future self would say to you today after quitting something that isn't meant for you. How would your future self look back on this season?

CHAPTER **22**

FREE INDEED

There are times when I am overly undone by the Lord's abundance in my life. I'm sitting here writing the last chapter to my first book in my early twenties, in the middle of graduate school, and working in an amazing career field. I've been cheered on by the best support team I've ever had in my life, and these beautiful people were never in the plan or what I thought I deserved. I'm learning God's abundance comes when I abandon the notion God *should* be for me. Instead, I'm finding abundance is where I discover more about Him and His wild calling for me. When my focus shifts from me to His glory, I find my calling advances because it's not about me anymore. Psalm 34 illustrates this realization:

> *The young lions suffer want and hunger; but those who*
> *seek the Lord lack no good thing.*
> Psalm 34:10, ESV

When we focus on the Lord first instead of our own satisfaction, we have the assurance of goodness and abundance. We have the promise in front of us we will lack no good thing, and that is motivation for our wild calling. I've learned in order to seek abundance, we have to be willing to take a few steps each day to find Him in every moment. I'm an extremely "to-do list" based person, so if you're like me (or even if you're not), I hope these will be helpful for you! Here are five things I've learned to practice doing as I walk this wild calling.

The Wild Calling

One. I had to keep praise on my lips in order to fight the fear I was not enough. By actively using worship as warfare to push back fear, I'm able to combat lies from the enemy with worship lyrics and scripture. For me, this can be through singing or writing out Bible verses and putting them throughout my home.

Two. Seeking the Lord's voice starts with a simple, ongoing conversation with Him. When I drive down the road, I talk to Jesus. It can be something as simple as asking Him for help and guidance as I'm on my way to work, or it can be a prayer for blessing as I drive by a church or school. When we keep conversation going with God, it can make it easier to hear His wild calling.

Three. I've learned when my emotions flare up, I weather the storm when I take refuge in Jesus. When I start to feel frustrated with a friend or loved one, taking that emotion to Jesus before anyone else, is the key to glorifying Him in the middle of an emotional storm. In this wild calling, we can keep things a lot more rational if we bring them to the Father first.

Four. I had to develop a healthy fear of the Lord. Yes, I believe a healthy fear of the Lord is a beautiful thing. A healthy fear of the Lord is where the spiritual gift of discernment can grow, and discernment is so important to figuring out what God wants us to do.

Five. I have learned that when I guard my words towards others and seek God's peace in every situation, I will see difficult situations or relationships with strife resolve into peaceful ones. By asking the Lord daily how to respond to others, I find myself walking through life with less stress over what I say because, ultimately, that will come from the Lord.

After reading all of these things, please don't think I have it all figured out. Abundance is hard, and living this wild calling is not always a beautiful ride. It's hard to feel like you deserve God's goodness when all you see is your shortcomings. I thought I didn't deserve a happy relationship, a peaceful home of my own, and beautiful people to run this race with. God blows me out of the water every day with His goodness, and it's like drinking out of a fire hose. I'm not satisfied with this life; I want a daily taste of the Kingdom more than I want oxygen.

FREE INDEED

Abundance comes from realizing the goodness of God in your life today and then asking His double portion on tomorrow, all the while, humbly submitting to others. Abundance is not the excess of good things, but rather, it is the goodness that the Lord provides. God is good, and His abundance is mind blowing. In Genesis 18, two extremely important stories take place. In the first, God reminds Abraham and Sarah of the promise He gave them of a son. Sarah does not believe God has this abundance in store for them and laughs to herself. In John Calvin's commentary on this passage, he makes the statement the promise was repeated specifically because Sarah needed the assurance it would come to pass.[22] By her hearing the promise directly from the angels, she was assured it would come to pass. God wasn't repeating this promise as a way to tease Abraham and Sarah or prolong their waiting but to issue the reminder He is a good and kind giver of abundance.

When I question God's abundance in my own life, Genesis 18:13-14, reminds me nothing is impossible when God's timing is what I'm depending on.

Then the Lord said to Abraham, "Why did Sarah laugh and say, 'Will I really have a child, now that I am old?' Is anything too hard for the Lord? I will return to you at the appointed time next year, and Sarah will have a son."
Genesis 18:13-14, NIV

I can sometimes stop before God's abundance is complete because I'm willing to settle for the "good" of the season I find myself in, instead of constantly seeking God for His "best." The second half of Genesis 18, has driven something home for me: when I have a relationship with God, I can have conversations with Him about His abundance for my life and see Him work.

Abraham had a close relationship with God, and God used that friendship to bless Abraham abundantly. When I ask God to do something mighty, I have to ask from a place of friendship and not impatience with His timing. When it comes to Sodom and Gomorrah, this section of Genesis 18, is a teaching lesson between God and Abraham, with God using Sodom and Gomorrah as a way to show Abraham destruction was necessary. Their grievances were great, but Abraham begged God for redemption, and the dialogue started. He asked God for the sparing of the righteous and made known that he did not want someone to suffer unjustly.

Abraham was not trying to teach God His duty, but he petitioned that God not deviate from righteousness by unjustly killing someone who deserved to be spared. This is necessary to mention, as it helps the reader understand the full nature of God and His immense love for His people. God wasn't trying to unjustly destroy or harm righteous people, and He's not going to start now. If there is a heaviness or a hard thing in your life in which you are seeking God's relief or release, just know you're nowhere close to being finished on this journey. There is grace to be found when we realize that through the lens of friendship and closeness with God, all makes sense. Mission, vision, and purpose are found in God's grace. Go forward, and believe what you carry. The promises are not being withheld, and we will not be shaken as righteous members of the Kingdom. You can trust God with all you have, and with that outlook, your wild calling will make sense.

When you hear the word freedom, where does your mind go? John 4 talks about the Samaritan woman at the well who found true freedom by being seen by Jesus for the first time.

> *Just then his disciples returned and were surprised to find him talking with a woman. But no one asked, "What do you want?" or "Why are you talking with her?" Then, leaving her water jar, the woman went back to the town and said to the people, "Come, see a man who told me everything I ever did. Could this be the Messiah?"*
> John 4:27-29, NIV

Her past, present, and future were all seen by Jesus, and He saw her as loved. Being seen by someone and loved for who we are frees us from shame, just like the woman at the well. This is the good news of the Person who calls us on this wild journey. We are seen as loved by our Maker, and it all makes sense when that title is the one we cling to first. The Jesus who walked with the woman at the well is the same Jesus that walks with us today. When I need a reminder of this, I run to the Word, because when we get lost on our wild calling, we have to look to the Bible. It is our burning bush in times where we are looking for direction in our lives. Ultimately, when we look within ourselves for direction, we will get lost and disheartened. When we use the Bible as a guide on our wild calling, it tells us about God and how He directs us to walk.

Reading through the book of John and studying it in depth has given me a whole new look on the heart of Jesus. I've watched Him grow into His own calling, walk with tenderness and authority, and move in mighty ways on behalf of His people. He was strong, but kind, tough but compassionate, and willing to give all for what the Father had called Him to do. When we forget who we are and begin to walk with a burden, we must remember that Jesus was born of a woman but was fully God-the God who seeks us out, frees us up, and calls us toward glory. We can't look back on what we were, because if we do, we'll miss the glory of God in our midst today and every day moving forward.

One of the biggest things that has held me back from pursuing my own wild calling has been discouragement. I was so caught up in making people proud of me, I let the parts of me I was proud of die a little bit. Having a season where I felt completely trapped by other people's desires for my life has made me so thankful for the freedom I've found in Jesus. Thankfully, I found encouraging friends who reached into the pit I had found myself in and spoke truth into my dried up heart. They knew the words of a resurrecting God, and they anointed me with those words. For those people, I am forever thankful. I had wrapped my calling up in my occupation, my skills, and my gifts. While all these are wonderful things, they are not the source of our wild callings. I was the "yes girl," people pleasing my life away under the banner of Christ. Now, I'm so blessed to live life speaking words of resurrection to others. When it comes to living for the gospel, we can only output to the capacity to which we have received. We are called to live free so we can free others up for their wild calling. Therefore, if I'm caught up saying *yes* to everyone but myself and God, I'm enslaved by the constraints of a very full, people-pleasing schedule instead of the wild calling on my life. When I think of words of life and freeing other people for their calling, I think about John 4 and the words Jesus spoke to the woman at the well.

The Wild Calling

The woman said to him, "Sir, you have nothing to draw water with and the well is deep. Where do you get that living water? Are you greater than our father Jacob? He gave us the well and drank from it himself, as did his sons and his livestock."
John 4:11-12, NIV

As someone who has learned to trust Jesus by seeing His hand in my life time and time again and asking what He was teaching me, I realize that I've asked Him a lot of questions along the way. I've left situations where I didn't understand why I should leave, only to figure out that God's hand was on my situation all along. I've walked away from so many things the world deemed beautiful and fulfilling in order to pursue the wild calling. If you're struggling to figure out how to discern yours, let me help you light the way with God's truth. One of the things I look for when God asks me to trust Him is the hint of a promise in the Bible that relates to my season. While it doesn't work all the time, I have walked away from times with the Lord with a pocket full of promises to claim over my life. I've gotten words of encouragement, adoration, healing, hope, and covenants so precious that I can never forget them.

One promise I'm carrying for the rest of my days is the covenant of salt from the Old Testament as discussed in earlier chapters. At the time I learned of this promise, I was dealing with doubt that God was providing or holding me close, and I was beautifully reminded that He had promised me this covenant. As Christians, we have access to these promises, and if we seek the Lord's face, we can find ourselves experiencing a covenant of closeness and provision with the Lord. On this journey of wild calling, look for trails of salt as you run your race. They will remind you God is working. Let His calling be the flavor you have on your life and let Him be the friendship you desperately seek for all of your days. As you finish this book, know I have prayed over you this beautiful Hebrew prayer:

Chazak, chazak, venit-chazak.
"Strong, strong, let us be strengthened!"

Be strengthened in your wild calling, my friend. This is a beautiful journey when we believe what we carry. Do not look back. There is glory to be found on this wild calling adventure.

Reflection Questions:

1. What voices have you listened to over God's voice in this season?

2. How are you seeking out the promises of God for your life?

3. As we come to the close of this book, know that I am praying over you that God would reveal these beautiful aspects of your wild calling for the rest of your days. In looking back since you started this book, what have been some of the main things God has taught you?

Final Thoughts

I've always loved lists. Rules to follow, tasks to accomplish, or my next steps. If we've learned anything throughout this book, it's that God's wild calling isn't always neat and tidy, but it is freeing. So, to keep with my list-making heart while simultaneously giving myself space to watch God work, I've come up with the Wild Calling Mantras. It's a collection of statements to encourage you in your wild walk with Christ. Feel free to add your own, and get ready for the next wild adventure God has for you.

As Wild Calling people, we say yes to the adventures God has for us, full of confidence in His love. When fear or untruths come to the surface, we reject them in the name of Jesus. Our lives have a Heaven-bent course to them, and we are ready to surrender every aspect of them for God's glory. Our work, schedules, and relationships are all His, and while this requires bravery, it is so worth it. As Wild Calling people, we lean into the idea, we aren't made to please everyone, and even in the middle of despair, there is hope. Change is the nature of God, and He has called us to witness it and be moved by it. Wild Calling people have an idea of the next adventure God calls them to, realizing they've been freed from guilt and despair for His purpose. Lean in, hold fast, and buckle up. This wild calling is our birthright to claim, and here we stand in the wide open spaces of God's grace and glory, shouting our praise.

THANK YOU'S

Abba, this wild calling has been beautiful. I can't wait to see where you take me next. Help me to remember I was created for such a time as this. I'm not looking back; there is glory here. You are so good, and I'm so abundantly thankful for Your wild calling on my life.

My beautiful family, thank you for cheering me on in ways I could have never imagined. Dad, thank you for teaching me how to love people with fierce loyalty. I will always be thankful for the way you cheer me on. Mom, thank you for anointing my head with oil every single day. I will never be able to tell you how your prayers have blessed me. G, thank you for preaching to my heart on days when I didn't know what God's voice sounded like. Redemption is amazing. Mam, Paula, Chris and my whole family, thank you for believing in me through this whole journey. I am eternally grateful for the love you've poured out through it all.

Em, thank you for the photos and for the encouragement that the person in them was beautiful (even when I didn't feel or see it). You are magical.

My gal pals: thank you for prayers, tears, and everything in between. Thank you for every text, call, and for walking this wild calling with me.

To every friend at West Towne, thank you. You've welcomed me with open arms and taught me how the church should love. It is like honey to my soul, and I love you all dearly. The Lord is doing so many wonderful things in this body of believers, and I am so excited to be a part of it.

To every person on my launch team and every person who has called, texted, prayed or encouraged me: I could not do this without you! Thank you for all you've done for me. I pray this book blesses you one hundred fold.

To Emily, thank you for being the most fearless "chaos-organizer" I know. You jumped into my mess with grace and humor, and I wouldn't have been able to launch this book without you.

My publishing team, thank you for the kindness you used to edit my words, the grace you used to cheer me on, and the fun we had along the way. You all are some of the best people I've ever met. I will forever give you all the credit for getting this book launched and published.

Notes

1. Goff, Bob. Everybody Always: Becoming Love in a World Full of Setbacks and Difficult People. Nashville, TN: Nelson Books, an imprint of Thomas Nelson, 2018.

2. "'ΣΥΝΤΗΡΩ' English Translation," bab.la. Accessed June 3, 2020. https://en.bab.la/dictionary/english-greek/sustain.

3. Isaiah 44:3

4. Jeremiah 4:31

5. Isaiah 11:8

6. Isaiah 28:9

7. Esther 3:13

8. Psalm 8:2

9. Isaiah 7:14

10. 1 Samuel 16:18, Proverbs 1:4, 7:7, 20:11

11. Psalm 10:14, 82:3, 146:9

12. Isaiah 9:6

13. Isaiah 31:9

14. Proverbs 22:6

15. Oxford dictionary. "Delight." Accessed June 3, 2020. https://www.lexico.com/en/definition/delight.

16. Rowe, Mike. "'Learning from Dirty Jobs.'" www.ted.com, 2008. Accessed June 3, 2020. https://www.ted.com/talks/mike_rowe_learning_from_dirty_jobs/transcript?language=en.

17. Adam, Adolphe. 1847. O Holy Night. Public Domain.

18. Oakeley, Frederick. 184. O Come All Ye Faithful. Public Domain.

19. Young, Sarah. Jesus Calling : Enjoying Peace in His Presence. Nashville, Tennessee: Thomas Nelson, 2019.

20. Pankhurst, Jennifer. The Conventions of Biblical Poetry. 2018. Accessed June 3, 2020. https://www.myjewishlearning.com/article/the-conventions-of-biblical-poetry/.

21. Morgan, G. Campbell. Searchlights From the Word. Eugene, Oregon: Wipf & Stock Publishers, 2010. Reprint.

22. Calvin, John. Calvin's Commentaries: Commentaries on the First Book of Moses Called Genesis. Grand Rapids, Michigan: Baker Books, 1974.

About the Author

Savannah Price is based out of Knoxville, TN, where she works as a Residential and Commercial Realtor, attends graduate school at Covenant Theological Seminary, and serves as a worship leader. She graduated with a Bachelor of Science in Digital Marketing and Advertising and used that degree to build and then sell her marketing company. She has served in many facets of ministry inside and outside of the church, and this is her first book from United House Publishing.

You can visit her website at www.thewildcallingbook.com or follow her on social media @savannahbprice.

CPSIA information can be obtained
at www.ICGtesting.com
Printed in the USA
JSHW051942250621
16250JS00006B/148